Found in Translation
Common Words of Uncommon Wisdom

Pamela Jay Gottfried

for Risa,
I am so grateful for your
steadfast support & friendship!
חג אורים שמח!
לכידתו —

Hanukkah 5771

Cover illustration ©2010 Susan Lubliner. Interior artwork ©2010 Loren Stein Designs. Author photo ©2010 David Barrack.

Typography and book design by Corey-Jan Albert.

ISBN 978-0-557-76336-8

For my parents

A Note about Pronunciation and Transliteration

One of the most daunting tasks of writing and publishing this book was transliterating Hebrew and Yiddish words into English characters. The reason such work is complicated is that English has no phoneme which corresponds to the guttural sounds of these languages. This sound is pronounced like the final sound in the surname of the composer Johann Sebastian Bach, and is represented by the 8th and 11th letters of the Hebrew alphabet.

It is common practice to use a "ch" to identify this guttural sound, without distinguishing between the two letters in the Hebrew alphabet. But in academic circles, the "ch" is eschewed because it is imprecise and misleading to those who would pronounce the "ch" as in "Charlie." The academic convention of using the ḥ to identify the *ḥet* (the 8th letter of the alphabet), and the kh to identify the *khaf* (the 11th letter of the alphabet) is certainly preferable, and I have adhered to this rule in the bracketed pronunciation guide for each essay. I have chosen, however, to preserve the "ch" spelling in several words, because they are commonly spelled in English with a "ch" and they looked strange to me without the "ch." Having departed from my academic training and rendered inconsistent English spellings throughout the book, I ask you to remember that when you read an essay with *italicized* or **bold words** containing a "ch" it is pronounced with a guttural sound, as in Bach. I hope this association helps you enjoy the music of the language!

Table of Contents

Introduction: The Gift of Words

I know that I am not the only adult who remembers that special teacher who made a difference in her childhood. I was in third grade, and I was a real bookworm. When I would come across an unfamiliar word, my mom would tell me to "look it up," so I spent a fair amount of time perusing the dictionary. Sometimes, my classmates would tease me for "using big words." But my teacher, Mrs. Ivirio, recognized my vocabulary as a gift rather than a liability, and she encouraged me to develop into the voracious reader that I am today. She also taught me how to use my words to nurture relationships with others and to share my enthusiasm for words with those around me. More than thirty years later, her influence changed the course of my adulthood.

It was the summer of 2006 and I was working at The Weber School, a Jewish community high school in Atlanta, which was moving from trailers into a new building. After protracted negotiations, the city inspectors gave us approval to occupy the building just days before the opening of school. In the early morning on the Friday before Labor Day weekend, the entire faculty and staff arrived to get the classrooms ready. Although the school employed many non-Jewish staff, we knew that the building would be closed at sundown for the Jewish Sabbath and we would not be permitted to finish our work until Monday. Mildly panicked, we found ourselves racing against the clock. As we were unpacking boxes, dragging half-empty cartons from one room to another, and wondering how we would accomplish this formidable task, I casually mentioned to another teacher that I had never *shlepped*[1] so many boxes in one day. "Is that Yiddish?" she asked. Her question left me momentarily speechless.

As a native New Yorker, I had assumed that the whole world knew Yiddish. From a young age, I was interested in William Safire's explanations of Yiddish words that have become commonplace in English over the years. Living in Atlanta, I continued to read *The New York Times* religiously, working the crossword puzzle and never missing Safire's "On Language" column. When I taught in a Jewish day school in New York, I discovered that even the non-Jewish teachers possessed a basic Jewish vocabulary. It had therefore never occurred to me that my colleagues in Georgia found themselves at a linguistic disadvantage in our daily conversations.

---

[1] See page 15.

My friend's question led to my realization that much of what we say to each other gets "lost in translation." Occasionally, this occurs because an unusual word slips into the daily speech of those who know many languages. Yiddish, in particular, is a rich language with a host of words that are at once versatile and virtually untranslatable. Some of these words have crept into English dictionaries, but most are not typically found in daily conversations that take place outside of Jewish circles. Yet many Hebrew, Yiddish, and even English words represent universal concepts. Imagine if we could incorporate them into a common language, providing us access to more colorful descriptions of the mundane actions in our lives, like *shlepping* cartons when we move to a new place. As I settled the box onto a shelf in the Biology lab, I knew that one of my roles as the school's rabbi would be to teach the faculty new words, to create a common language among our diverse group that would enable us to communicate and work together. We needed an "inside lingo" that would unite us in our efforts to inspire our students to learn.

That afternoon, I emailed the answer to my friend's question in a brief essay, and launched my "Word-to-the-Weber-Wise" project. I began walking the halls of the new building, listening for words to share each week with my colleagues. Many essays, inspired by the daily routines of our life at school, sparked conversations in the faculty lounge and led to ongoing discussions of our mission as teachers. As adults working in an educational environment, we were committed to our own life-long learning. The non-Jewish teachers wanted to connect to their Jewish students and colleagues, and were eager to share their newly-acquired vocabulary. The American-born Jewish teachers were eager to connect to the language of their immigrant grandparents and to the native language of their Israeli-born colleagues. Several teachers asked me to include English words, as well, that expressed our shared values. I was privileged to contribute to our professional growth and development, as time and again I was reminded of Mrs. Ivirio, who had been my mentor in sharing my love of words with others. This book is a culmination of two years of nurturing relationships with my colleagues, one kind word at a time.

Naturally, the most meaningful aspect of this project was personal, not professional. In creating the weekly essays, I was able to grow as a wordie, collecting new words even as I revisited the familiar ones of my childhood. Unable to locate Mrs. Ivirio, who was no longer teaching at P.S. 52 in Staten Island, I was fortunate to reconnect with another of my favorite childhood influences, my dad. He grew up in Brooklyn speaking Yiddish to his immigrant parents. Together, we returned to the language of his youth, throwing around Yiddish phrases and debating nuances of particular words. We laughed a lot, as we made editorial decisions about what to omit, noting that some of the most colorful Yiddish words and expressions would not be suitable for the project. If I called my dad on Thursday afternoon, he knew we would be talking about words, and he helped me make almost every Friday deadline. This project brought us closer as adults, enabling me to *hock* him *a tchainik*,[2] as I now wish I had when I was younger. *Found in Translation* is a gift of words from an adult child to her parents. I am grateful to be able to share it with you.

---

[2] *Hock a tchainik* is a Yiddish phrase meaning talk a lot, yammer, or yak. Literally it means to knock a teapot or kettle, which I guess approximates the sound of a chatterbox.

Targum (Hebrew) תרגום [**tar**-goom]
noun: translation

As a proper noun, the **Targum** refers to an Aramaic translation of the Torah. This translation was driven by the people's need to feel connected to the text, and was largely a necessity in a time when few people understood Hebrew but virtually everyone spoke Aramaic. In our day, as in theirs, the need for real connection is paramount, and the desire for a common language to express ourselves is sacred.

Bubbemeises
Family, Philosophy and Folk Religion

Bashert (Yiddish) באשערט [ba-shert]

adjective: destined, predestined, fated, meant to be, inevitable. Sometimes used as a noun to mean one's soulmate.

It is a human, universal need to explain that which cannot be explained. When faced with a mystery, a puzzle, or a question, we crave meaning, solutions, and answers. Yet there are many things that defy our understanding. When confronted with an inability to make sense of the universe, it helps me to believe in God and to trust in God's plan. I don't doubt that many religions developed in response to this need for faith.

Perhaps I am lucky to have been raised in the folk religion of Eastern European Jewish immigrants to believe that everything is **bashert**. When I was in rabbinical school, Jewish Philosophy professors were quick to judge this as an unrefined theology. Still, even then I knew that faith does not originate in the head but in the heart. Believing that some events are simply predestined can offer comfort when the questions we ask cannot be answered. In fact, no professor or rabbi has been able to provide a more definitive answer to the difficult questions that I have posed about faith. However, the unsophisticated belief that everything is **bashert** has been the foundation of a steadfast loyalty to God for many generations of Jews. It can't be all bad then, can it?

In addition to teaching me the belief in **bashert**, my dad was careful to instill in me that all we can control is our reaction to those things beyond our control. A self-deprecating sense of humor can be a powerful tool when wielded during life's challenging moments. "Man plans and God laughs," according to the Yiddish proverb. Living with life's uncertainties – the surprises, challenges, disappointments – is certainly easier when we are able to imitate God and laugh as unexpected events spoil our well-laid plans. Though my father did not claim to learn this life-lesson from reading the works of great thinkers, it is attributed to Albert Einstein who was also an Ashkenazi Jew.[3] In Einstein's estimation, the ability to accept our lack of control will protect us from losing our good humor. With laughter comes acceptance that some of our plans may go awry. That is almost certainly **bashert**!

---

[3]Ashkenazi Jews are of German or Eastern European descent.

Emes (Yiddish) אמת [em-es]

noun: truth; *adjective:* true, correct

My grandfather left Russia for New York, hidden on a ship up to his neck in a barrel of oil. This is was an incredible story which I heard as a child – and I mean, truly incredible, as in "not believable." But its retelling was always followed by someone saying "*Dos* is the **emes**!" which loosely translates as "It's really true!" This phrase is usually said after one tells a story which contains slight exaggerations or embellishments. It's a kind of disclaimer, a reassurance that we are serious about the story's message even if we may have taken liberties with some of the details.

I recently asked my dad to verify the facts about my grandfather's immigration to the United States. What he could tell me, on the record, was that my grandfather traversed what was then Red Russia to the Baltic Sea and took a ship to the east coast of Canada. He then traveled to Toronto, came south through Westchester, NY, the Bronx, and finally arrived in Brooklyn. My dad recounted the tale of his father hiding in a barrel on board the ship. "*Dos* is the **emes**!" he insisted. "A barrel filled with oil?" I asked. "I never heard that," he replied. "That must have been on your mother's side."

There is no one else to ask about my grandfather's travels. He died before I was born, and none of his generation is still alive to say "*dos* is the **emes**." I suspect that even if he were here to say it, I would only partly believe him. I imagine that he made his circuitous journey because he believed that a better life awaited him in America. Perhaps his dreams of religious freedom and prosperity propelled him forward. I cannot know why he came or what he encountered along the way. I know only the stops in his itinerary – the year he became a citizen, the city in which he married my grandmother – and this series of facts does not nearly comprise the significance of his life story. *Dos* is the **emes**.

In court, witnesses swear to tell "the truth, the whole truth and nothing but the truth." But advances in forensic science have taught us that eyewitness accounts are often unreliable. An individual's sworn statement may be true in his or her mind, but it's not necessarily the **emes**. The human pursuit of truth, a single truth, is idealistic – this truth is unattainable. In reality, the story that we create about the journey, *dos* is the **emes**.

4

Ima (Hebrew) אִמָּא [ee-mah]
noun: mom, mommy

When I look in the mirror I see my mother. I knew that this would happen eventually, as I have always borne a strong physical resemblance to her. I was unprepared, however, for the extent to which I would become her as a parent. As I navigate the waters of mother-child relationships as **Ima**, I can finally appreciate the lessons I learned about motherhood from my mom. [4]

When I was a teenager, my mother would often say "someday you'll have a daughter just like you." Back then, my friends thought my mother was cooler than their own, because she would talk to them, ask them questions, express interest in their lives. Back then I was mortified. Now I am **Ima,** and she is *Savta*, grandma. Now she admits that her parental blessing was only partly fulfilled. "She's just like you, only smarter," my mom proclaims about my teenage daughter. My mom and her first grandchild share an uncommon relationship and, occasionally, a common enemy.

As **Ima**, I find myself repeating the parental blessing and other things my mom said to me to my eldest. Whenever our strong-willed and independent personalities clash, she rolls her eyes at me and says, "You were much worse! I've heard stories from *both* of your parents." I ask a question that she deems too personal and she employs the silent treatment for the entire afternoon. Later, when I am already in bed, half asleep with a book in my lap, she wants to tell me everything about her day. I remember torturing my mom in this exact way. I scoot over so that she can sit down next to me while we talk.

My younger daughter prefers to talk as we walk the dog together. She is truly an all-around competent child, but she sometimes worries that she has still not figured out what her "thing" is. She has tried art lessons and track team, drama and Girl Scouts. As **Ima**, I am able to model flexibility and patience for her thanks to my mom, who developed new interests, as well as her career, in her late thirties.

---

[4] My decision to have my children call me **Ima** was not really a conscious one. From the moment of the birth of my eldest, I spoke to her, sang to her, read her stories and taught her nursery rhymes in Hebrew. Having struggled for Hebrew fluency at the age of nineteen, I was determined to give my children the head start that I had missed. When I referred to myself, as parents often do with small children, in the third person, I was **Ima**. This was unremarkable when I was raising my daughters in New York City, a city of polyglots, but a bit more unusual for my son, who is a native Atlantan.

She in turn inspired me to pursue new ventures in my late thirties, including training for an endurance walk and taking a pottery class. With the support and encouragement of my mother, and my mothers-in-law, I took a sabbatical from my teaching to pursue other career goals. I reassure my daughter that she has the potential to develop any of her interests with passion and dedication when she is ready. I listen with awe as she describes her excitement at reaching the top of the climbing wall at camp, delighted that she has excelled at this activity, one that I have not yet attempted.

My son sits across from me on the floor, a game board between us, and chats. One afternoon, a friend of mine telephoned during a particularly never-ending game of Monopoly, and he quickly became impatient to resume playing. When I asked to call her later, she said that she was impressed that I make the time to play with him. I marveled at her comment, because I believe that a perk of motherhood is having an excuse to revisit the games of childhood. True, it isn't always possible to carve out the time to play, nor is it easy to relegate cooking dinner and folding laundry in order to be fully present for the entire game. But I remember playing endless games of Scrabble with my mom and brother, long after we were old enough to entertain ourselves, and I know that this is a priority of my being **Ima**.

Carpooling and board games, silence and late-night conversations: These are the gifts that my mother gave to me years ago, long before I would inhabit the body of **Ima**, long before I would see her face in my mirror. I delight in unwrapping these gifts for a time and then carefully retying the ribbons, knowing that my children will someday appreciate the opportunity to unwrap them, too.

Kadima (Hebrew) קדימה [ka-**dee**-mah]
adverb, colloquial: Forward! Onward!

In its many verb forms, the Hebrew root k-d-m can mean to precede, to come early, to anticipate, to be the first, to have priority over, to advance, to go forward, and to make progress. With one simple expression that connotes so much about movement and progress, Hebrew proves to be a rich and nuanced language. Perhaps the Jewish value of "getting somewhere in life" is a vestige of living in the Diaspora for nearly 2,000 years and desperately trying to return to the Promised Land. For an exiled people, moving onward means heading toward home.

A downside of this constant striving for progress can be restlessness. Some of us cry "**Kadima**!" because it is difficult for us to wait. We are accustomed to forward motion, so taking the time to stop, to reflect, to pause and enjoy the moment can be a challenge. Perhaps our wandering as a people has contributed to our impatience, as well.

In our post-modern era, it is not only Jews who are transient. Our sense of time and place is always shifting, as ideas and information move at breakneck speed across oceans and continents. People are no longer bound to a single place; we are even free of the confines of the earth's atmosphere.

The Hebrew language recognizes the inherent timelessness of movement by deriving the words for "moving forward in time" and "looking backward in time" from the same root. **Kadima** is where we are headed, the future days; *y'may kedem* are the days of yore, the ancient days. These two idioms suggest that time is cyclical, and that true progress encompasses the best of what has already happened. Sometimes, when we feel that we have stalled out, it might help to remember that movement of all types – forward, backward and lateral – can lead us onward in our journeys.

Thus, I am often inspired to shout "**Kadima**!" and to listen for others shouting, too. I am restless to get moving. There is always much to accomplish, with many days behind us and the days ahead too few. But I will also try to be patient, to pause, to cherish each moment. **Kadima**! Let's get moving: We still have so many important journeys to make.

Livriut (Hebrew) לבריות [lee-vree-**oot**]

colloquial: response when someone sneezes (*literally:* to health)

I was sitting in a meeting with a group of teachers when someone sneezed. A polite colleague immediately said, "God bless you!" and then asked me if Jews say this to one another. Well, of course we do – we Jews are steeped in folk religion as much as anyone! Some ancients believed that when a person sneezed, the soul was temporarily expelled from the body, and so the person's need for protection was both immediate and urgent. As a child I remember hearing that the origin of this social convention was the belief that one's heart stopped momentarily during a sneeze. I always wondered why we didn't say "God bless you" for a hiccup, which seemed to me a far more serious malady.

Why in Hebrew do we say **livriut**, "to health," rather than "God bless you?" In many languages, I know this is the case. My dad always blessed us in Yiddish when we sneezed: "*Zegazunt*" was his way of pronouncing "Go in health." This resembles the German "*gezund heit*," and also reminds me of the Spanish "*salud*." So many ways to ward off another sneeze and acknowledge our desire for good health!

I think there is an essential difference between wishing God to bless us and wishing each other good health. While we sometimes cannot control our health, we do have power over how much we give in to feeling under the weather. Our minds and our words can help us to combat a mild cold. I hardly know a teacher who takes a sick day over the sniffles. We consider our time in the classroom too precious to waste on languishing over a mere virus. Instead, we fill our mugs with tea and boldly claim that it's more important to teach. Who has the time to wait for a cold to run its course?!

During the winter, even in the temperate climate of Atlanta, many mothers of young children struggle to exert our will power over the flu and other ailments. For a few months, the cold, rainy weather takes a toll on our generally strong immune systems. Mothers don't have time to be sick, so we persevere through the day – going to work, driving carpools, cooking meals and going to evening meetings at school and synagogue – sounding vaguely congested and looking a bit less perky than usual.

So, why do we press on through the sneezes, wishing each other continued health? I believe that we are taking a stand against the common cold, striking a pose of imperviousness to human frailty. **Livriut** is an earnest expression of our determination to keep our hearts and minds active during our bodies' momentary lapses of strength.

Mazel (Yiddish) מזל [**mah**-zl]

noun: luck; from the Hebrew *mazal,* planet.

"Mazel tov!" literally means "good planet," though we use it in ordinary speech to say "Congratulations!" When your luck is good, it is as if the planets are in their proper alignment in the sky. But when the universe becomes improperly aligned... well, sometimes *"oy!"* is the only thing to say when your luck abruptly changes.

I remember a particularly wonderful morning: I taught a great class, recited lovely and heartfelt prayers, drank a delicious second cup of coffee. But after lunch my **mazel** changed. First, I raced past a speed trap as I was running late to a doctor's appointment. Without sharing too many specifics about my encounter with the law, I can say that the officer was not charmed by my winning smile and earnest apology. He took his time writing up the ticket, until I felt a mild pressure building behind my eyes, and I realized that I was going to be more than a few minutes late.

Driving away, I glanced at my cell phone, wondering whether to call the doctor's office to postpone the appointment for another day. Of course, the battery was dead – even though I had recharged it overnight. Merging onto the highway, I noticed that the mild pressure had advanced to a dull throb. I finally arrived at the doctor's office, with a full-blown headache, only to discover that a computer glitch had erased my appointment from the roster. "Don't worry," the receptionist said. "If you can wait, we'll work you in by 2:30." Taking a deep breath, I sat down to wait, wistful for the morning's **mazel,** and faintly suspicious that my earlier experience that day was actually a fabricated memory.

There are people who go through every day much like A.A. Milne's lovable, but perpetually depressed character, Eeyore, with a black rain cloud hovering over their heads. Their stocks are always down, their spouses are always neglecting them, and their bosses are always cranky. When my dad would mention a friend who could never get ahead he would say, "That guy's got no **mazel**," with a vague sense of pity, but also a touch of wonderment. How could someone go through life with nothing going quite right? As luck would have it, their planets never orbit the sun; the sun never shines for them. Such people are called, in Yiddish, *shlemazel,* which loosely translates as "the guy whose waiter always spills the soup on him."

I believe that the best antidote to Eeyore's cloud is an umbrella. Sometimes you've just got to make your own **mazel**. The errant cell phone battery was a nuisance, but it was also a reminder to drive with both hands on the wheel, and one eye on the speedometer. The hour-long wait at the doctor's office was an opportunity to read the latest issue of a magazine. It was a gift of time: time to sit still, time to allow my head to clear and my adrenaline to abate. I was not surprised to find that by the time I arrived home in the late afternoon, my **mazel** had changed once again. I was relaxed and ready for whatever the evening had in store for me.

Mishpochah (Yiddish/Hebrew) מֶשְׁפּחה [mish-**puh**-ḥeh/mish-pah-ḥah]
noun: family

"You can't choose your family." This was the time-worn adage
in my family, often repeated when I balked about something I
just couldn't stand about my brother, or my parents, but especially
my brother. Now, as an adult and a mother of three, I can finally
appreciate the wisdom of this saying.

My children are so different from one another that it can be
challenging to nurture a sense of belonging to the same **mishpochah**.
One strategy my husband and I employ to create strong bonds among
us is "family dinner." Almost without exception, we eat dinner together
every night. This custom has posed its own challenges, because at our
family table there usually sits one picky eater at any given time. Since
my husband and I agreed early on, when our eldest was a toddler,
that we would not fight about food, we taught her to make herself an
alternative if she did not like what was served. With our guidance she
learned to make healthy choices – peanut butter sandwiches, yogurt,
cereal – and she learned that she could go several days without eating a
hot dinner. I learned not to worry about her eating habits, and when her
siblings began to go through phases of picky eating I stopped keeping
track of who was eating what which week. But my son, who simply
adores his older sisters, knows their favorite foods, along with all their
other favorites. When he heard that I had made baked macaroni and
cheese one night, he shouted triumphantly: "Good! Maital likes that,
and she will finally get to eat dinner!" Not only did he know his oldest
sister's preferences, he was genuinely happy that her needs were being
met. This is what it means to be **mishpochah** – to be ultimately happier
when your siblings are also happy.

Mishpochah isn't only a nuclear family, of course; it also refers to
the extended family. When my mother was a child, she was fortunate
to have holiday celebrations with the "cousins club" that included
nearly 100 people. That was back when the entire **mishpochah** lived
in the same neighborhood. When my husband and I moved our
children to Atlanta, a city in which we were both offered jobs, we
were disappointed that we had no family here. But over the years we
learned that **mishpochah** isn't limited to family, but includes the friends
who become like your family. We worked to create a local family that
rivals our actual **mishpochah**, currently scattered across the Midwest
and up and down the eastern seaboard. My Atlanta **mishpochah** now

consists of people who are listed as our emergency contacts, who stop by unannounced when they are driving past our house, who call if they haven't spoken to me in a few days, even if I have recently emailed them or updated my Facebook status. It is not only our blood that binds us to our **mishpochah**, but also our shared values and genuine affection.

I respect my parents for raising me to value family ties and to balance my individual needs with the competing needs of my family members. I believe that is has helped me as a parent raising three individuals within one family. I feel fortunate to have maintained strong relationships with people who knew me as a child and to have cultivated deep friendships as an adult with people I have met only recently. It is true that you can't choose your family and that you are stuck with them for life. In a sense, though, when you welcome new friends into your life, you can choose to expand your **mishpochah**.

Pekele (Yiddish) פעקלע [peck-eh-leh]
noun: package, parcel, bundle

My grandmother always had a collection of shopping bags in her front hall closet. She stuffed them in there after *shlepping*[5] them home from the neighborhood stores in her native Brooklyn, and she packed them full of leftovers when we visited for dinner. Her bag rule, like her Tupperware rule, was that if you returned it empty she would refill it for you. My first memory of the word **pekele** was as a reference to one of those bags.

The better-known usage refers to the metaphoric **pekele** that each of us carries with us. This connotation of **pekele** is so common that it appears in the Yiddish-English dictionary as "burden" or "bag of troubles." In English we might call it our "baggage." What do we keep in a **pekele**? We shove frustration and disappointment in there, difficulties we are experiencing, personal issues that we don't want to share – and we carry it everywhere. Sometimes we use what's in there. Sometimes the bag leaks. Mostly we just carry it around, thinking that it's heavier than everyone else's **pekele**, imagining that our lives would be perfect if we could just get rid of it. But that bag has staying power, like the ones in my grandma's front hall closet.

One lesson of the **pekele** is this: Your **pekele** is unique. No one else can really feel how heavy it is, because only you can carry it. You can never trade your **pekele** for someone else's – nor should you ever want to do such a thing. If you believe that your **pekele** is filled with the heaviest burden, then it is time to regain perspective. According to my grandmother's wisdom, God only fills your **pekele** with what you can carry.

Another important lesson of the **pekele**: If you are fortunate enough to find ways to share its contents with compassionate friends, they can relieve you of some of its weight. True friends remind us to put the **pekele** down for a few minutes and stretch our arm muscles as we regain our strength.

---

[5] See next essay.

Shlep[6] (Yiddish) שלעפּ [shlep]
verb: to carry, drag

I made some discoveries about myself during my sabbatical year, especially in those first weeks away from the daily demands of classroom teaching. The quality of time spent working at home is strikingly different, and I relished being in control of how I spent the hours that my children were at school. When I picked them up at afternoon carpool, however, the pace of my day usually changed. For a mom who works at home, each day offers a new opportunity for driving endless miles or for doing laundry, and sometimes for both. I found that I needed to devise a job title to reflect my main activity. I prefer **Shlep**-Exec to Soccer Mom: It has a certain ethnic flair. Besides, my kids don't play soccer.

Shlepping is the duty of every mother I know. Kids growing up in the suburbs require rides everywhere – to school, the library, after-school lessons – until they are old enough to drive themselves. Then we begin to wish that we were still doing the driving because waiting for them to return home is so stressful! Kids also produce an incredible amount of laundry, which seems to increase exponentially in their laundry baskets from the moment the clean clothes are folded and placed in their drawers. While the **shlepping** of motherhood can test one's mettle, the years of our children's utter dependence upon us are so fleeting that I always try to see the upside.

Although the word itself, with its strong bilabial "p" sound, can seem a bit negative, **shlepping** is not necessarily a bad thing. When one **shleps** so many baskets of laundry up the stairs that she can barely stand up straight, she cannot avoid *shvitzing,*[7] and that can help balance out the extra calories she consumed while packing the kids' lunches in the morning. **Shlepping**, when it refers to traveling a long distance, often gets you somewhere, as in "I have been **shlepping** from one end of Atlanta to the other looking for kosher marshmallows." In this case, it is also permissible to use the noun form, as in "It's such a **shlep** from my house to Toco Hills," where the kosher markets are

---

[6] I have followed the YIVO Institute for Jewish Research standard when spelling Yiddish words in English, e.g., shlep instead of schlep, shmooze instead of schmooze. To hear the Yiddish alphabet read aloud, visit their website at www.yivo.org.

[7] Sweating. See page 38.

located. This particular **shlep** has a positive outcome for my entire family, because it enables me to serve hot cocoa with marshmallows on the one day a year that school is closed due to snow. A word of caution: It is not polite to use the noun to refer to a person, unless you wish to compliment a child for helping you with the laundry, as in "Shira is a star-**shlepper**: She carried all seven loads of laundry upstairs! She deserves a raise in her allowance."

You have to be careful with Yiddish words, because two words can sound alike yet be very different. **Shlep** is a verb that refers to the physical realm. But if you drop the "l" from this word, you will have a verb that connotes deep emotion. We **shlep** laundry up the stairs, which can be enjoyable, but the feelings resulting from our physical exertion are beside the point. We *"shep nachas,"* which means we derive tremendous pride and pleasure from our children's accomplishments. Lose the "l" and you gain access to true joy in witnessing the growth and development of the next generation. I hope that we continue to *shep nachas* from our children long after the time of **shlepping** them and their laundry has passed.

Tuches (Yiddish) תחת [**tooḥ**-iss]
noun: rear end, buttocks, tush

I love spring! By the time Passover is finally over, I've been sitting on my **tuches** for nearly six months, worrying about how it is spreading widely beneath me, wondering when I'm going to be ready to walk ten miles and if I'll fit into my summer wardrobe in June. Following eight days of filling my belly with *matzah*,[8] I'm ready to get off my **tuches** and exercise!

There is probably not a more versatile word in the Yiddish language than **tuches**. It figures in so many idiomatic expressions that it would be impossible to recount them in one essay. I decided to focus on my dad's favorite: **tuches** *afn tish*, which loosely translates as "put your money where your mouth is," or more literally as "put your rear end on the table."

Whether it's about meeting a deadline – such as the spring tax deadline – signing a contract, returning corrected midterm papers, or registering kids for summer camp, **tuches** *afn tish* communicates the importance of making a commitment and following through in real time. During the dormant months of winter, it is easy to put off unpleasant tasks and to forestall even pleasant activities, knowing that spring is generally accompanied by a burst of energy. After all, to procrastinate is human. Putting your **tuches** on the table can require the courage and strength of a superhero.

In the final weeks of a school semester, teachers may feel compelled to teach this expression to their students, especially to one who is suffering from spring fever or senioritis and may need to get his **tuches** in gear. Parents may feel tempted to deliver a *patshn tuches*[9] to their children, and even those who eschew such drastic disciplinary measures will find that, despite their philosophical views, *patshn tuches* sounds terrifically threatening as a consequence for non-compliance. Your kids may not know what you are saying, but they will take your Yiddish words seriously!

Finally, we would all be wise to bear in mind that weekends are a time for settling your **tuches** into a comfortable chair and reading the paper, doing a crossword or Sudoku puzzle, watching a baseball game and relaxing, so that you are ready to face the coming week with the requisite strength to put your **tuches** *afn tish*!

---

[8] Unleavened bread

[9] Slap on the behind

Ani v'Atah
Living in Community

Fair (English)

adjective: without irregularity or unevenness, e.g., a fair playing field;
verb: to make the connection or junction (of surfaces) smooth and even.

In the fall of 2007, Gregory Chase, a 27-year-old hedge fund manager from Nashua, NH made headline news. In what seemed to be a publicity stunt, Chase offered NBC one million dollars on behalf of former Alaska Senator Mike Gravel, to allow him to participate in the Democratic presidential primary debate. I must admit that I was initially suspicious about Chase's motives. I also admit to being troubled by the fact that he spent nearly $500,000 to place ads in national newspapers – newspapers that during those same weeks reported that more than 500,000 people had been displaced from their homes by wildfires in southern California. But I tried to listen to Chase's story with an open mind, and I was moved to hear him describe his actions as an attempt to achieve a **fair** playing field in the election process. He persuaded me that NBC's denying access to a candidate whose ideas could inform the debate and whose presence could positively impact the election process was unfair. Gravel may not have raised sufficient funds to be a true contender in the race, but we might still benefit from NBC allowing him to make himself heard. Chase certainly raised his voice in support of **fair** play, and forced me think about the issue of fairness. How often we hear the complaint, "it's not **fair**!" The phrase, "*zeh lo fair!*" has even crept into modern Hebrew, despite several ancient roots that convey fairness, justice, and righteousness.

Kids and teens tend to think of issues as black-and-white, and they struggle with recognizing the gray areas. Something is right or wrong, good or bad, **fair** or unfair. Teachers and parents of teenagers face daily challenges in persuading them to look at issues from multiple perspectives, to see beyond their indignation when something seems wrong to them. At the same time, their perspective is valuable – they remind us that life can be unfair, that the world is not always a **fair** place. I tend to have a knee-jerk reaction to the phrase "it's not **fair**," so I am learning to hear it differently, to appreciate that I must examine an issue that has been labeled "unfair" more deeply.

According to several etymological dictionaries, the word **fair** originated as a verb, and was used in ship-building to mean: "to make level, to adjust the lines of the hull, to correct curvatures." This connotation of **fair**, to **fair** the hull, restoring it to its proper form, really resonates for me. "It's not **fair**" can be a complaint, but it can also be a reminder that we must make adjustments, aligning a situation so that it is smooth and balanced. In restoring the word **fair** to its original meaning, we can expand our understanding of the world and see more clearly the irregularities that need to be faired.

Gibor (Hebrew) גִּבּוֹר [gee-**boor**]
noun: hero; *adjective:* strong, mighty, courageous, valiant

When I donated platelets for the first time, the American Red Cross recruiter insisted that I take a gift, an insulated coffee cup that reads "Platelets Hero" under their logo. I accepted sheepishly – I didn't feel the least bit heroic. I was just an ordinary donor, offering what little I could to alleviate our city's blood supply shortage. In fact, when I saw the size of the needle I felt downright cowardly, and I looked away.

The word **gibor** evokes in me thoughts of the righteous citizens of European nations who hid Jews during the Holocaust; the rescue workers who ran into the towers on 9/11; the nurses who stayed with hospice patients in New Orleans during Hurricane Katrina. Usually when these people are asked about their heroic deeds, they claim to be ordinary people simply doing what needed to be done. A true **gibor** is almost certainly someone who does not regard himself or herself as extraordinary.

Along with humility, there is another characteristic of a **gibor** that is conveyed by the Hebrew root in the verb *l'hitgaber*, to overpower or overcome. War heroes are hailed for overpowering the enemy. Ordinary heroes, in contrast, courageously overcome their own circumstances. Like those mentioned above, everyday heroes choose to act when human nature would allow them to yield to inaction. It is easier to ignore unpleasantness, to look away rather than confront a difficult situation. Do we not consider soldiers stationed abroad, who face daily violence and instability in their work environment, to be heroes? How much more so is the soldier who brings water to civilians waiting at a border checkpoint in the unrelenting, summer heat? This **gibor** cannot abide the suffering of another person, even if that person is his sworn enemy. This **gibor** refuses to succumb to his circumstances, military service in a region of ongoing conflict. Instead, he summons the strength to act – quenching another's thirst, extending an olive branch.

The ancient rabbis[10] taught that a **gibor** is one who conquers his own nature, the human nature that allows us to focus on our own

---

[10] Whenever I write the "ancient" or "early" rabbis, I am referring to the sages and teachers of the early rabbinic period of Jewish history (first century B.C.E. through first century C.E.), who were responsible for interpreting the biblical laws and created a wealth of Jewish legal texts and traditions that were handed down through the centuries.

needs while ignoring the needs of others. The **gibor** is not a mighty hero who vanquishes his enemy, but an individual who possesses the strength of character to overcome the bystander within himself. A **gibor** recognizes the humanity in another person and is strong enough to embrace it.

Ḥaver (Hebrew) חבר [ḥa-**ver**]
noun: friend (*alternative spelling:* chaver)

Friend (English)
verb: to invite someone to join your social network on Facebook

I had to chuckle when the following message appeared on my Facebook Wall: "Pamela is now friends with _____." The name in the blank belonged to someone I have known for close to ten years. We used to work together, and I think she still has some of my maternity clothes in her closet. We are now Facebook friends – or rather, I have **friended** her. A few days later, a friend called me to set up a lunch date and she asked me, "How do you have so many friends already? You've only been on Facebook for a week!" "I wouldn't say that I have so many friends," I replied, "it's just that I know a lot of people."

I remember during my teenage years, when girls changed from best friends to mean girls in a heartbeat, my grandma often told me that a person should be able to count her true friends on one hand. She would say this to comfort me whenever a friend betrayed my trust, gossiped about me or ignored me to talk to a boyfriend. But she herself observed her rule of five only in the breach: My grandma never met a stranger. She collected friends; they were drawn to her because she was honest, kind and compassionate. Though not a Hebrew speaker, my grandma understood the many nuances of **ḥaver**.

A **ḥaver** is so much more than a friend. A **ḥaver** is a colleague, someone who shares your values and supports you in your endeavors, who inhabits your professional world and is a member of your community. A **ḥaver** is also a **F**riend with a capital "f,"[11] a boyfriend or lover, who occupies a special place in your heart. A **ḥaver** is more than an acquaintance – a true **ḥaver** will share with you and sacrifice for you, because you maintain a depth of commitment to one another. In one of its many verb forms, this Hebrew root means to be united or connected. A **ḥaver** is an abiding friend, who stays connected to you always.

Recently, I reconnected with a woman I knew in high school after finding and **friending** her on Facebook. Somehow, I wasn't surprised that speaking with her was not awkward at all. We just picked up

---

[11] It is notable that since the Hebrew language does not contain uppercase letters, it is impossible to distinguish in writing the difference between a friend and a "Friend." This distinction can only be made through use of facial expressions and tone of voice.

the conversation where we left off twenty-five years ago. Another friend, who I knew professionally many jobs ago and who happens to be old enough to be my mother, called this week to see how I was doing. Same story: We ran out of time long before we had used all our words. My husband marvels at how I can talk to anyone. My relationships don't recognize the typical barriers of age, gender, social status, political views, and religious affiliations. These friendships transcend time and place, enriching my life in unexpected ways.

I am grateful for my friends, and thankful to have more than five, even though this violates my grandma's rule. I believe that it is imperative to nurture friendships with people who knew you before you were who you are today – the ones who know your old nickname and your eccentric habits, the ones who don't notice your bad hair or who are honest enough to point out the piece of food stuck in your teeth, the ones who love you despite your many foibles, the ones who remember your birthday and don't care that you forget theirs every year. A **ḥaver** brings the joys of life into sharper focus and blurs the pains until they have dissipated. These kinds of friends are essential – they provide a sense of continuity in life, connecting the past as it rushes into the future.

Ḥen (Hebrew/Yiddish), חֵן [**ḥayn**]
noun: grace, charm, beauty
The name Hannah is an Anglicized, feminine variant of this word.

Studies in evolutionary biology have shown that human beings indicate a preference for symmetry. More specifically, we are programmed to regard those with symmetrical facial features as beautiful. Any parent who is making monthly payments to the orthodontist can attest to this beauty ideal. Nevertheless, I do not consider symmetry to be the measure of a perfect smile. Instead, I find the depth of feeling behind the smile to be the outward expression of a person's **ḥen**.

I knew a woman with such a smile, one that projected her inner beauty, warmth and charm – her **ḥen**. When she smiled, she transmitted those qualities to those near her, making them somehow more beautiful. When she was alive, her pure **ḥen** influenced other people to behave more kindly and to speak more gently. She fought a long and painful battle with breast cancer, but throughout her protracted illness she never acted sick; the disease was unable to diminish her **ḥen**. After she died, many people who were inspired by her way of living honored her memory by walking in the Susan G. Komen 3 Day Walk for the Cure. One walker, in particular, made a lasting impression on my soul. When I asked him about his connection to her he told me simply that she was his client. Mike is a personal trainer, a short muscular guy with somewhat nondescript facial features. But when he smiled as he remembered their relationship, he emanated such warmth; he was truly filled with **ḥen**.

Ḥen is often translated as grace, which to an English speaker's ear can sound Christian. Jews don't often speak of God's grace, but we should. The charm, beauty and warmth signified by **ḥen** is really best translated as grace, an aspect of our humanity bestowed upon us by a divine source. Perhaps to be created in God's image is to embody God's grace. One of our responsibilities, then, as human beings is to radiate **ḥen** with every smile.

Ḥesed (Hebrew) חֶסֶד [ḥe-sed]
noun: kindness (*alternative spelling:* chesed)

With so many of our business transactions relegated to the realm of the Internet, I was surprised to find myself recently inside the Post Office. I needed to buy 26¢ stamps, which were not available for purchase from the machine in the lobby. When I arrived, I was a bit surprised to find the line snaking its way around the room to the entrance. I sighed to myself and assumed the "waiting stance."

Just then an elderly man walked past me toward the exit. Burdened by two canes and leg braces, he was moving pretty slowly – more slowly than the line. A woman, from near the front of the line, darted into action. "I'm just going to get the doors for him," she said to the woman behind her as she passed. This Post Office has a set of glass, double doors, and they are heavy and inconvenient for someone who does not have use of two arms.

Suddenly, the line began moving. One person bought a sheet of stamps, another mailed a single package. "She'll never make it," I heard someone behind me mutter. I looked back. She was still holding the first of the double doors open as the man dragged himself along. There were now five or six people behind me, who had no idea that this woman had left her place to help a stranger. I allowed myself, for just a moment, to imagine that one of them would balk at her return to the front. Then I silently scolded myself for assuming that people would be less generous of spirit than this situation required.

As the elderly man exited the building, a puff of cold air worked its way inside. The woman returned quickly to her place and a few people smiled at her. "Next in line, please," the man behind the counter called out. Her place-holder laughed and said, "Good timing." The woman smiled and shrugged. "He needed some help with those doors," she replied. Then she stepped forward to the counter, ready to conduct her business.

I often fear that we have become inured to **ḥesed**. We spend so much time alone, seeing only our computer monitors, hearing only what is piped directly to our ears through our headphones. It is possible to function in our society for days without ever speaking to another person. If I go months without waiting in line at the Post Office, how often am I missing opportunities for **ḥesed**?

28

This woman's kindness wasn't really a big deal to her because it is innate to her personality. But I kept thinking wistfully that you just don't get to see interactions like that every day, and I was grateful to have witnessed this spontaneous act of **ḥesed** while running my errands.

Ḥevra (Hebrew) חברה [ḥev-rah]

noun: society, association, company (*alternative spelling:* chevra)

On some level, the word **ḥevra**, from the root word h-v-r, meaning "friend," defies translation. It is more than a just a group of friends or associates. It is a cohesive collection of diverse individuals, who are united by a common purpose. The feeling that I get from being in a **ḥevra** is an almost indescribable sense of wholeness. Perhaps I can best illustrate the meaning of the word by relating the story of a special group that I am privileged to call my **ḥevra**. I joined this society of Sunday walkers in July 2006, when I was training for the Susan G. Komen 3 Day Walk in Atlanta.

From January to June I walked alone or with my canine companion, Jenna. But in July, when my weekend walks began to exceed ten miles, it became clear to me that I needed to find a **ḥevra**. It is not good, nor is it always safe, for a woman to walk alone. The 3 Day Walk website provided a schedule of training walks, where I found a group meeting before dawn on Sundays in Roswell Area Park. I wasn't looking for a long-term commitment – it was just three months until the Walk – and I was ready to meet some interesting people who shared my training goals. I was totally unprepared for the ways in which joining this **ḥevra** would change my life.

Our weekly conversations began as a comparing of notes: which socks best resist moisture, where to buy sneakers, when to stretch hamstrings, how to raise $2,200. They developed into a sharing of life stories: who was walking to support a friend with breast cancer, who was honoring the memory of a sister, who was celebrating ten years of remission. One especially hot and humid day, when we all looked and felt pretty awful, we distracted ourselves by planning to meet for dinner in November, dressed in normal clothes and wearing make up. Walking really frees people to talk about all kinds of things. At first, we talked constantly. Later we shared comfortable silences, too. I began to look forward to waking up at 5:30 a.m. on Sundays and driving to Roswell in the dark.

In August, we realized that we needed to step up our training schedule to include back-to-back walks. I had anticipated this conversation and decided to encourage the group to walk without me, since my observance of the Jewish Sabbath prohibited me from driving on Saturday mornings to meet them in Roswell. The women were especially interested in my religious observance, and asked probing questions about my refraining from driving or carrying money on those days. Instead of allowing me to walk alone, my ḥevra began meeting me in my neighborhood every Saturday morning. Whenever we stopped at gas stations, my friends bought too much water or sports drink for themselves, and they insisted that I allow them to pour some into my bottle. I should have realized that members of a ḥevra are dedicated to one another.

They called me their rabbi and I taught them about Judaism. Yet, week after week, I learned from them. We often prayed together on those mornings. We prayed in silence for the women we walked to honor. We prayed aloud for the strength to make it up the hills. We prayed with our tears and we prayed with our feet. I could never have predicted, never have imagined, that being part of this ḥevra of walking women would renew my faith.

Several weeks after the Walk, shortly after Thanksgiving, our ḥevra met for dinner. One by one we hugged each other and laughed about how great we all looked wearing normal clothes and make up. We were reunited, no longer sharing *only* a sense of purpose, but, more importantly, a deep affection for one another. Our association was borne of sweat and blisters, and tears of both joy and sorrow. Our acceptance of our challenges and celebration of our accomplishments strengthened our resolve to meet for monthly walks, to reaffirm our sense of ḥevra at regularly-scheduled intervals. Laughing and nodding in agreement, we decided that ten miles is just the right distance for catching up on news, sharing ongoing conversations and praying with our feet.

L'hitraot (Hebrew), **להתראות** [l'heet-rah-**ote**]
colloquial: See you again! So long! (*literally:* to see each other)

When I was younger I used to think that my dad was odd because he never said "goodbye." Even now, when he hangs up the phone at the end of our conversations he always says "so long." As a child, goodbyes never fazed me, but over the years I have grown to dislike them. Now that I am an adult, my dad's trademark "so long" really resonates for me.

The Jewish goodbye is famous for taking several hours. This is not merely a cultural quirk, but the result of an almost-mandated custom. The Jewish laws concerning welcoming guests include a variety of unusual traditions, among them the custom of seeing a guest to the door. When a guest leaves your home, you are instructed to step over the threshold with him as he leaves, to indicate your reluctance to see him go. Allowing a visitor to see herself out is forbidden, and anything less than an hour devoted to her departure seems disrespectful. This goodbye is a kind of dance intended to make the guest feel valued.

The Israeli goodbye, in contrast, is more casual. Like the French who favor *au revoir*, Israelis simply say **l'hitraot**. Perhaps because it is a small country and people tend to see each other often in the streets, markets and parks, it seems more reasonable to say "see you again!" **L'hitraot** as a parting greeting has an optimistic, hopeful quality to it. It reminds me of how Jewish people depart from weddings and funerals, saying *"rov simchas,"* which loosely translates as "let's meet again at happy occasions."

Nowadays, when I say goodbye to my parents, I am aware that they will not live forever, and that any time I say goodbye may be the last time. My friends, too, live all around the world, and I rarely have an opportunity to see those I left behind in cities where I used to live. Having lost several loved ones to cancer, I don't take "the next time I see you" for granted when I say **l'hitraot**. Yet I am infused with a sense of optimism and hope. Our parting may be permanent, but I doubt it. I try to remember to imitate my dad and say "so long," because it may be a while before we see each other again. Still, somehow, I trust that when we meet again it will be a happy occasion.

Manhig (Hebrew) מנהיג [mahn-**heeg**]
noun: leader (*plural:* **manhigim**)

The Hebrew language is so compact in nature that from one root, n-h-g, a family of words meaning to drive, lead, direct, conduct, and behave are all derived. These words connote various meanings when the root is conjugated in different ways. **Manhig** is its causative form; in its simplest form, *nahag*, it means driver. Like many American Jews traveling in Israel, I learned the word *nahag* riding city buses in Jerusalem, because people would scream it when they wanted the driver to stop at the next corner.

What then, beyond grammatical construct, is the essential difference between a bus driver and a leader? The bus driver follows a prescribed route. He makes important decisions – about speed and stopping distance – but only within a system that he did not devise himself. A leader directs a team of city planners, engineers, environmental scientists, mechanics and other personnel required to create the transportation system itself. A **manhig** can fill the room with his or her presence, rallying others to work toward a common goal. A **manhig** can also work behind the scenes to effect change. A **manhig** inspires others with vision, creativity, high standards, and consistent kindness.

Although **manhigim** wear a variety of faces they often bear a striking resemblance to one another. One leader hides in the darkness of the theater wings and allows an ensemble of talented actors to take center stage. Another leader, mature beyond her years, shares her vision and creativity with an audience left breathless by the beauty of her art. Still another leader, who often stands quietly in the background, takes a step forward and inspires others to walk beside him. Finally, one brilliant leader takes a step back to reflect upon the meaning of her work, and demonstrates the importance of replenishing one's own spirit in order to serve others with a full heart.

Perhaps you have seen these **manhigim,** encountered them as you go about your daily business. But it is also possible that their actions escaped your notice. In my experience, true leaders are often humble people, sharing the credit with those who support them. To be a **manhig** is to conduct oneself with purpose and direction in all undertakings, large and small. A *nahag* drives a bus through a neighborhood; a **manhig** is a driving force within a community.

Rachmanes (Yiddish) רחמנות [ruḥ-**mun**-es]
noun: compassion, sympathy, mercy, pity, empathy

Showing compassion for others, having true empathy, is not easy. Not because we are insensitive or selfish, but because we are creatures rife with inconsistencies. Often, we show a public face while concealing our weaknesses, which we generally prefer others not to see. Yet, my experience is that we are unable to hide them completely. People have "tells" – a quivering lip, fidgety hands, lack of eye contact. These behaviors are usually not in our control, and often betray inconsistencies that lie beneath the surface of our faces, our words. When I notice another person's "tell," I am reminded that I must have **rachmanes** for her.

One spring a new student enrolled in our pottery class. She seemed to be perfectly "normal," maybe in her late 20's or early 30's; it was hard to judge her age. She talked about her husband and her daughter, and how she had taken pottery many years ago and already knew the basics. But something about her was strange. What she was telling us definitely did not fit with what she was doing in class. Her tiny pots were like ashtrays; her hands were wobbly on the wheel. I felt the stirrings of sympathy for her, but not real **rachmanes**, because her behavior was so inconsistent with her words that it was hard to have a conversation with her. She was always in the studio when the rest of us arrived, and she seemed to have been waiting for a quite a while. But she never started working; she always waited for the teacher to arrive. Then, after an hour or so of the 2½ hour class, around 8 o'clock, she would clean up, pack up her stuff, call out goodnight to everyone and leave.

One evening, I finished earlier than usual, a little before 9 p.m., and I left. It was already pretty dark outside. I walked to my car and found her sitting on a rock next to the parking lot. Before I could even ask her if she needed help, a van pulled up alongside her, and the driver began shouting apologies for being late. She yelled back with enthusiasm (and maybe some relief): "It's okay, John! I always come out early to wait for you!" The side of the van read "Just People Village," a non-profit organization serving adults with special needs in Metro Atlanta. I felt a jolt of **rachmanes** hitting me full force in the *kishkes.*[12] She was developmentally disabled and was certainly aware that she had some limitations. But she hid her true self from the teacher and all of us students in the class. Hearing the joy in her voice as she bantered with the van driver, I recognized their true friendship – John knows her completely, and she doesn't need to conceal her inconsistencies or weaknesses from him. We hardly knew her at all. I swallowed back the tears that accompanied my guilt at having withheld **rachmanes** from another.

When can we trust each other completely to reveal ourselves, to rely upon each other for support and comfort? Maybe these fleeting glimpses of the hidden parts of ourselves are all that we are capable of seeing in one another. Yet, how can we have true empathy, how can we treat others with compassion, when we have no idea what pain lies beneath the surface, what needs are hidden behind impassive faces and polite conversations?

As I watched the van exit the parking lot, I was struck by the realization that we praise God for the attribute of mercy, **rachmanes**, for His creatures. We, as imperfect beings, can achieve only partial understanding and a small measure of sympathy for each other's pain and difficult circumstances. Perhaps the challenge of being fully human is to be willing to reveal the deepest parts of ourselves to others, and to emulate God by striving for true **rachmanes**.

---

[12] *Kiskes* are intestines. Here, "in the *kishkes*" means "in the gut." See page 69.

Shmooze (Yiddish) שמועסן [shmooze]

verb: to talk idly or casually, and in a friendly way, in order to make a social connection. *noun:* a chat, a warm heart-to-heart talk

We learn from reading the biblical story of the creation of human beings that we are essentially social creatures. Although there may be times when even the most sociable person among us needs some alone time, no one wants to feel lonely. So we are fortunate to have been blessed with the gift of language, which enables us to pursue the art of conversation.

In Yiddish, the particular conversation known as a **shmooze** has only one purpose; namely, to help us connect with one another. **Shmoozing** is not about imparting information or teaching a lesson. Instead, it is about the informal, face-to-face interactions that help us form social connections that cannot be established through talking on the telephone or texting. Eye contact, body language, physical proximity and touch are all essential ingredients of the successful **shmooze**. These chats are often about nothing special; the topic of conversation is secondary to its warm and casual tone.

Some might argue that **shmoozing** leads to gossip, which was strictly outlawed by the ancient rabbis. They classified any idle conversation to be a waste of precious time that could be spent studying or discussing Torah (Jewish Law). But I believe that **shmoozing** is actually valuable talking time in its own right; it is an important activity that nurtures feelings of connectedness and wards off isolation.

This is particularly true in a local synagogue where I sometimes attend Sabbath morning services. Casual Fridays may be relatively new in the American workplace, but Judaism has always regarded Shabbat, which begins on Friday and continues until Saturday evening, as the perfect time to relax and **shmooze** with one another. Recognizing the importance of **shmoozing** in building community, the rabbis and lay leaders there maintain the warm and social atmosphere that is the hallmark of this synagogue. Although talking during the prayers is not encouraged, there is always a luncheon after services. The regulars tend to stick around for a while, **shmoozing** over the last bottle of soda and a few half-eaten cookies. People may not remember what was discussed over lunch once they leave the building, but the warmth they feel about their fellow congregants carries them from week to week, until they can **shmooze** again. There is powerful truth in a casual conversation that inspires such a sense of belonging and community.

Shvitz (Yiddish) שוויצן [shvits-en]
verb: to perspire *Hebrew colloquial:* to brag

As a northerner who moved to the south, I was more than a little surprised to learn that the school year does not begin on the Tuesday following Labor Day. Here in the hot and humid south, school begins in August, during the hottest part of summer. Having heard a variety of explanations – none of which make any sense – I am convinced that no one knows the origin of the strange custom. I can only assume, then, that folks in the south are accustomed to having to **shvitz** in school.

It's not that I object to this human accommodation to heat. I find **shvitzing** useful when walking the dog and appropriate when working out at the gym. Health enthusiasts recommend exercise, steam baths and saunas to promote **shvitzing**, which they believe purges the body of toxins. I recognize that **shvitzing** is inevitable in the subway trains in New York City. I have even heard that drinking a cup of hot tea or soup on a summer day helps a person chill out, which always seems counterintuitive to me but really works, because it causes **shvitzing**. We humans are lucky to have bodies with natural coolant – perspiration. Not all animals were so ingeniously designed to withstand the heat. In the dog days of summer, while our canine friends pant, we **shvitz**.

I remember beginning one particular school year in an August of record-breaking temperatures. The school's central air conditioning unit could not keep up as the mercury climbed higher and higher, and as the week wore on teachers came to meetings wearing t-shirts and shorts. The principal left an extra blouse in her office, in case parents needed to see her in the week before classes began. Throughout the week, we sat in meetings, unpacked boxes, loaded text books onto shelves, moved desks, arranged chairs, rebooted computers, made photocopies and **shvitzed**. What choice did we have? Knowing that the students would arrive on Monday for the first day of class, wondering how they would concentrate in such weather, we tended to our work and prayed for a respite from the unrelenting heat. I still thought it was strange to start school in the middle of summer, but I was proud of how we teachers braved the weather to honor our commitment to the calendar.

To me, the best thing about the word **shvitz** is that is it also found in colloquial Hebrew, but it has a completely different connotation. In Modern Hebrew, **shvitz** means to boast or brag. A **shvitzer** is a braggart, which is generally an insult, but it can be socially acceptable to **shvitz** in Hebrew about the achievements of others, if not about your own success. Part of what motivated me to write this essay was the desire *l'hashvitz al ha-ḥaverim she-li*, to brag about my colleagues. And when our children make us proud, we are expected *l'hashvitz*, to share our joy in their accomplishments with others. If I wanted to translate this Hebrew word into a common Southernism, I could simply say that my children gave me reason "to brag on them." **Shvitz** is certainly a versatile word to have in one's Jewish vocabulary.

In Yiddish you **shvitz** when you're overheated; in Hebrew you **shvitz** when you're accomplished. We had good reason that August to **shvitz** in both languages. Thanks to the **shvitzing** of a group of hard-working professionals, or perhaps thanks to our fervent prayers, the heat wave ended as the school year began.

Yachid (Hebrew) יָחִיד [yah-ḥeed]

noun: single, sole, individual, alone, unique, isolated

It is no coincidence that **yachid**, which means individual, is derived from the same root as *m'yuchad*, special. Thus, the Hebrew language acknowledges that each individual has unique gifts, just as the bible teaches that each of us is created in God's image, that each of us possesses a spark of the Divine. So, how can **yachid** also mean alone and isolated? During my years as a high school teacher, when I was invited to be a guest speaker in a classroom for students with special needs, I caught a glimpse of this double-meaning. One student, whose diminished cognitive abilities were the result of a childhood brain tumor, connected with me in a moment when my heart was open. The moment was at once exhilarating and painful.

This student often struggled to communicate her ideas and feelings to others, but she excelled at decorating functional objects, such as pens and letter openers, with intricate beadwork. The process of choosing and attaching the beads challenged her to improve her fine motor skills, and engaging in her craft was therapeutic for her, as well. As a fellow artist, I felt connected to this student, as I, too, find fulfillment in the creation of functional artwork. Since I don't have any training in teaching students who are *m'yuchad*, I just talked with her as I did with other students, about her individual gifts and passions. I felt a responsibility to protect her against the isolation that is borne of silence; we often don't know what to say to someone who is *m'yuchad*. Her artistic talent is part of what makes this young woman special; it distinguishes her as a **yachid**. The greatest challenge of teaching may be finding a bridge to each **yachid**, knowing each student and discovering what makes each one *m'yuchad*.

As we got to know each other over the months that followed my first visit to her classroom, our shared passion for creating art continued to unite us. We worked together with other students on a number of fund-raisers, including a Hanukkah sale of her work – the proceeds of which were donated to the Brain Tumor Foundation for Children – and a bake-sale to raise money for a summer camp for children who have cancer. Recently, her parents have helped her develop a business, and she has begun to sell her work at art fairs and on her website. With each sale, she gives back to the organizations that helped her overcome the challenges presented by her illness.

It is also no coincidence that in Hebrew the word **yachad**, meaning "united" or "together," is derived from the same root as **yachid**, individual. In this instance, the etymology is completely logical and beautifully expresses the connections that can unite individuals. When **y'chidim** truly work together, **b'yachad**, no one can remain isolated or alone.

Yeshivah (Hebrew) ישיבה [ye-shee-**vah**]
noun: meeting

Many people are familiar with the Yiddish word *yeshiva*, and are used to seeing it spelled in English with a capital "y" as part of the name of a school. This word, Yeshiva, with the accent on the penultimate syllable, does refer to a school, often an Orthodox one, where students and teachers study traditional Jewish texts. Fewer people know the Hebrew word, **yeshivah,** which is pronounced with the accent on the final syllable and means a "meeting." Both words are derived from the same root word meaning "to sit or dwell." There are a few synonyms for the word "meeting" in Hebrew, but **yeshivah** is frequently used to refer to the kinds of meetings that we conduct in schools to plan activities, discuss curriculum design, evaluate student learning, and sometimes drink coffee.

The **yeshivah** is, for me personally, a challenging place to be. First of all, social convention dictates that a person must sit in a meeting, unless, of course, you are the one lucky enough to be leading the meeting, standing in front of all assembled. It's hard for me, and I believe for many teachers, to sit for long periods of time. That's why I chose teaching over a cushy desk job. Generally, a **yeshivah** that extends beyond forty-five minutes exceeds my concentration limit. I'm a kinesthetic learner – I need to be moving around and doing something to feel productive.

One-on-one meetings, especially informal meetings, aren't so bad. I love the **yeshivah** that takes place in the hallway, the doorway of a room, the parking lot. My favorite **yeshivah** is what I think of affectionately as the "walk with me" meeting, since those are my exact words when you ask me if I have a moment. These meetings do not run too long or exhaust my ability to maintain my posture in a straight-backed chair.

Nevertheless, I am occasionally delighted to have a rather lengthy **yeshivah**; one that is somehow different from the others, one that stands out in my mind as more purposeful, more productive, than the rest. These are meetings when I don't notice the passing time, as I sit among the busy people and noisy chatter in Starbucks. The agenda of these meetings varies: I could be making revisions to my book with a friend who possesses editorial flair or catching up with a former colleague who has moved to a new job. Sometimes it is good to slow down and savor a **yeshivah**. We must allow ourselves the time we need to get to know another person, to listen and to be heard, to dwell rather than merely sit in a meeting. This, too, is doing something, even if it does not entail movement.

Gut Shabbes, Gut Yontev, Gut Yor
Jewish Holidays and Rituals

Hamantashen (Yiddish) המן טאשן [**hum**-en **tosh**-en]
plural noun: triangular, fruit-filled pastries or cookies, eaten on the holiday of Purim. The singular is **hamantash**, but you won't hear it too often, because you can't eat just one!

Hamantashen inspire much debate. First, these goodies are considered pastries by some and cookies by others. Purists use yeast dough and prepare the filling from scratch. Poppy seed paste, prunes and other fruit fillings are fairly traditional. Other Jews use canned fillings, fruit preserves, apple butter and even chocolate chips. Some of us also use sugar-cookie dough, which is easier and faster to make. Talk about cutting corners...

Another source of disagreement is the origin of their name. They are best-known by their Yiddish name, which means Haman's pockets, but is often translated as Haman's hat. Now, if you don't already know about that guy, you can read the Book of Esther in the Bible and let me know if you find any references to triangular pockets or head-gear. I didn't find a single one, and I have read it a few dozen times in my life. This is probably why the Israelis, relying on their superior wit and wisdom, instead call these delectable treats *Oznay Haman,* namely "Haman's ears." I'm guessing that Haman had noticeably pointy ears, rather than a tricorne. That makes sense, since the Romulans, who also have pointy ears, destroyed the Second Temple in Jerusalem. Or was that the Romans? I get confused on Purim. Anyway, I once taught a group of fifth graders the Hebrew name for **hamantashen**, and a droll boy asked me, "If the cookies are this creepy guy's ears, does that mean the filling is his earwax?" Since then I have not been able to eat apricot-filled **hamantashen**.

Finally, a favorite century-old quarrel to entertain Purim celebrants while they fulfill their annual intake of **hamantashen** is the Latke-[13] Hamantash Debate, in which contestants argue the merits of each of these calorie-rich, straight-to-my-hips holiday foods. Years ago I witnessed a debate between a Baptist Minister who favored oily latkes and a Reform Rabbi who tried to defend the honor of the sugary **hamantash**. That sweet, cookie-eatin' rabbi didn't stand a chance against the slick-tongued, fried-food lovin' minister. Still, the rabbi persuaded me to unload the contents of Haman's pockets into my gullet in order

---

[13] Latkes are the deliciously-fried potato pancakes traditionally eaten on Hanukkah. They are fried in oil to remind us of the Hanukkah miracle: According to rabbinic lore, a single cruse of oil was sufficient to keep the *menorah* (lamp) burning for eight days in the Temple following the Maccabees' victory over Antiochus IV. I love latkes year-round, as my hips, and God-willing not my arteries, will attest.

to *weigh* the merits of his argument. As we gastronomically-motivated Jews know, whether they are savory or sweet, holiday foods are the essence of any proper celebration.

Don't believe a word of what you read in this essay. Instead, try these recipes and then stage your own Latke-Hamantasch Debate!

Grandma Minnie's Latkes

5 large Idaho potatoes, peeled	1/3 cup flour or matzah meal
1 large onion	1 tsp salt and ¼ tsp pepper
2 eggs, beaten lightly	plenty of oil for frying

Using a 4-sided grater, grate the potatoes and onions. Strain mixture through sieve, pressing out excess liquid. Allow liquid to settle. Transfer potato/onion mixture to a bowl. Add seasoning, flour and eggs. Pour off the liquid and add potato starch to mixture. Drop roughly 2 tbsp of batter into a heated skillet with ¼ inch of HOT oil. Fry! Yield: 40 latkes.

Hints: Do not overcrowd skillet; do not turn until brown (approx. 2 mins.). Remove and drain on paper towels. You may warm in 200°F oven while you fry up the rest of the batter, but it's preferable to eat them as soon as you can do so without burning your tongue. Serve with applesauce or sour cream, or sugar, depending upon your family custom.

Beth Levine's Hamantashen

2 cups flour	1/2 tsp salt
1/2 cup sugar	1 tbsp orange juice
2 tsp baking powder	1/2 cup butter (softened)
1 egg	1 tsp vanilla

Suggested fillings: Apple butter, fruit preserves, thick jams, chocolate chips

Preheat oven to 375° F. Cream butter, sugar, eggs together. Mix dry ingredients in a separate bowl. Mix orange juice and vanilla in a cup. Add 1/3 flour mixture to sugar mixture. Add 1/2 orange juice/vanilla mixture slowly and mix. Repeat this process until all ingredients are fully mixed. Roll out the dough to 1/4" thick. Cut out rounds and add a spoonful of filling in the center. Fold the circles into triangles, pinching the edges firmly. Place on greased cookie sheet and bake until lightly brown (15-18 minutes).

Yield: 20 hamantashen

Ḥametz (Yiddish/Hebrew) חמץ [ḥa-mitts/ḥa-**mayts**]
noun: leaven, yeast (*alternative spelling:* chametz)

On the new moon, or Rosh Ḥodesh, that marks the beginning of the Hebrew month of Nisan, we start the two-week countdown to the seminal holiday of Pesach (Passover). In preparation for the week of eating *matzah* and celebrating the freedom from slavery in Egypt, it is Jewish tradition to rid our homes, our offices, even our cars of **ḥametz**. The early rabbis' preoccupation with the complete removal of **ḥametz** from our possession is indicative of one of two things: Either they were oblivious to the hassle of Passover cleaning because they were not personally responsible for scouring the oven and lining the refrigerator shelves, or they were legislating beyond physical **ḥametz** to include spiritual **ḥametz**.

The words derived from the root ḥ-m-tz not only mean leavened, but also mean fermented, sour or spoiled. For example, *ḥometz* (vinegar) is only palatable if mixed with other ingredients and used sparingly. The word *ḥamotz* means oppressed. This sense of the word **ḥametz** is certainly more relevant when we discuss its removal from our possession. How can we celebrate the holiday of freedom from slavery without purging the sourness which enslaves our souls? On Passover, there is no room in our homes or in our hearts for acidity. In preparation for Passover, we must rid ourselves of spiritual **ḥametz** in order to be truly free from self-inflicted oppression. This, by the way, includes the self-imposed rigors of spring cleaning. Women in particular tend to overdo it when removing the physical **ḥametz** and then find themselves exhausted during the late nights of the Passover Seder celebration. If we redirect our energy to clear out spiritual **ḥametz** we will fuel ourselves for the entire week of Passover.

Passover is the celebration of spring, a time of renewal and new beginnings. Trees and flowers are in bloom, blades of grass are poking through to soak up the sunlight – arrogance, grievances, and resentments spoil the flowering of spring, and prevent us from realizing its rebirth. While it is true that **ḥametz** causes flat grains to leaven into delicious, round loaves, **ḥametz** also puffs up a person until there is no room in his or her soul for joy. With two weeks to prepare, we can certainly find time to cleanse ourselves of all **ḥametz**, and find the true joy of freedom from our burdens as we welcome the arrival of Passover.

Kushya (Hebrew) קוּשְׁיָה [koosh-ya]
noun: difficulty, problem, objection (*plural*: **kushyot**)

Did you ever notice how Jews tend to answer a question with another question? If you ask a rabbi a question, there is a good chance that he or she will, instead of answering your question, pose other questions in order to engage you in a deeper conversation. Rabbis' responses often sound like this: "Could you clarify what you mean by that word?" or "Are there special circumstances in this particular case?" This potentially irritating habit probably has its roots in the text of the Passover Seder, the *Haggadah*, which begins with four questions that are never really answered.

These four questions are not actually questions at all. They are known in Hebrew not as the *arba she'elot*[14] but as the *arba **kushyot**,* and they begin with a single question: "Why is this night different from all other nights?" This is less a question and more an overall objection, a **kushya**, a difficulty or unresolved problem that the narrator has with the Passover ritual of the Seder. The person raising the **kushya** already knows that Passover night is different from all other nights, and he or she knows what makes it different. The main difference between a *she'elah* and a **kushya**, is that a *she'elah* generates an answer, and a **kushya** tends to generate more questions. In the *Haggadah*, the four **kushyot** that follow the initial question are a rhetorical device. They serve to call attention to the many ways in which this night is unusual and they indicate specific rituals that will be performed in the course of the evening.

In the Talmud[15], a **kushya** is an objection to a stated premise, which usually sets off a page or more of legal debate and interpretations. Here, too, the **kushya** provides an opportunity for more questions. It is a point of entry for the ancient rabbis in a sacred conversation. These sages were not argumentative; rather they adhered to rules of rhetoric that originated with the **kushya**. In many ways, a **kushya** is a signal to all participants in the conversation that the speaker has identified something worth discussing.

---

[14] The Hebrew word for a question is *she'elah;* its plural is *she'elot.*

[15] The Talmud is a 63-tractate collection of legal material and lore, comprised of the Mishnah (dating from 1st century B.C.E – 1st century C.E.) and the Gemara (4th- 6th centuries C.E.).

Truly meaningful exchanges begin not with agreement, but with unresolved difficulties. When we begin with **kushyot**, and we maintain a desire to reach mutual understanding and a commitment to hear the multiplicity of voices, then we are likely to continue asking more and more questions before we arrive at any answers. It is my prayer that our **kushyot** result not only in lengthy Passover Seder celebrations, but also in long-sustained relationships that are nurtured by our ongoing conversations.

L'shanah tovah (Hebrew) ‏לשנה טובה!‏ [l'shah-**nah** toe-vah]
colloquial greeting: "To A Good Year!"

On December 31st as midnight draws near, the words "Happy New Year!" are shouted into microphones at Times Square and sung out by children who were allowed to stay up later than usual for the celebration of New Year's Eve. It is an exuberant greeting of unfettered joy.

At Rosh Hashanah, the Jewish New Year, the mood is more solemn. Jews wish each other **l'shanah tovah**, a good year, rather than a "happy" new year. We choose the words of our greeting with care, as we try to express a sentiment that is both hopeful and truthful. Jews believe that the power to know the future lies only with God, and the power to affect the future lies within us. Thus, we begin the Jewish year by thinking about the previous one and determining how we can improve ourselves and our relationships through *teshuvah*.[16] There is nothing wrong with wishing for a good year or using the optimistic greeting of "happy new year." But as we convey our hopes to one another for a good new year, we acknowledge that goodness does not always convey happiness.

A good year may include difficult moments, challenges that must be overcome. Goodness is a result of struggling with the aspects of ourselves that we wish to change in the coming year. A good year may include discomfort, which is necessary for both learning and self-improvement. A good year may also include the comfort and kindness that we offer each other in times of sorrow. **L'shanah tovah** does not exclude the possibility that the year may bring loss and pain, as well as growth and development. Similarly, the wish for a "happy" year does not encompass the range of feelings that are necessary for goodness to fill our lives. Anticipating the year before us, we carefully consider our options and imagine the fullness in our futures. We say **l'shanah tovah** as a way of expressing our desire to experience the rich complexities of life in the coming year.

---

[16] Repentance. See page 62.

MiSheberach (Hebrew) מִי שֶׁבֵּרַךְ [mee she-bay-**rakh**/mee she-**bay**-rakh]
noun: prayer for healing (*literally:* "the one who blessed")

Many centuries ago, before the invention of footnotes and
bibliographies, the rabbis instituted a clever system of referencing texts
that was understood by the literate people of their day. They would
refer to a section or chapter of a book by its first word or words.
Today, we still identify the weekly Torah readings by their opening
words. Similarly, we call the prayer for healing by its first two words,
mi sheberach, and the list of names of those in need of healing the
misheberach list. While there are other prayers that begin with the
words **mi sheberach,** this shorthand is generally understood as referring
to the prayer for the sick.

The **misheberach** itself is straightforward, asking for healing of
body and spirit for those who are ill. In the middle of the recitation
of the prayer, the leader adds the names of those in need of healing,
or pauses to allow others to add their names. Many synagogues keep
a written list to use whenever the prayer is recited – traditionally on
Mondays, Thursdays and Saturdays when the Torah is read publicly,
which is considered a good time to petition God for help. It is also an
opportunity for the community to learn that someone is sick and may
be in need of a visit, a meal, or other assistance. Sometimes there is
nothing else for us to do but pray. Those of us who are not medical
professionals can feel pretty helpless when a loved one is sick, and
the **misheberach** provides us a moment of comfort. Hearing the names
recited aloud is a reminder that other people care.

There is a lesser-known custom associated with adding people's
names to the **misheberach**, and even those fairly knowledgeable about
prayer are not always familiar with it. Before the use of last names
became an established practice, Jews had been using their fathers' first
names as surnames. For example, I am called Tziporah the daughter
of Aharon. Now, although the use of surnames is commonplace, Jews
continue to be called by their fathers' names in synagogue rituals,
such as honors during the Torah service. In recent years, as egalitarian
practices became more widespread in Jewish worship, people began
to use both parents' names. I became known as Tziporah the daughter
of Aharon and Leah. But when people are added to the **misheberach**
they are referred to exclusively by their mothers' names. In the case of
this prayer, I would be called Tziporah the daughter of Leah. This is
the only instance in Jewish prayer, which tends to employ masculine

language, in which the mother's name is highlighted. Perhaps we rely on common wisdom that when you are sick you are your mother's child, regardless of which parent makes better chicken soup.

The **misheberach**, when taken together with a healthy dose of Jewish penicillin (i.e., aforementioned soup), is the spiritual prescription for a speedy recovery. In the presence of the Torah and the entire community, we pray that our **misheberach** list will be shorter next week, as those in need of healing find that God has answered our **misheberach** prayer.

Shamash (Hebrew) שַׁמָּשׁ [shah-**mosh**]
noun: central candle on the Hanukkah menorah (candlelabra), used to light the other candles (*literally:* server)

Shammes (Yiddish) שַׁמָּשׁ [shah-mess] *noun:* caretaker of synagogue, beadle; central candle on the Hanukkah menorah

Like many of you, I associate the word "server" with computer technology, as in "The server is down and no one can access email." However, the word **shamash** conjures up a different image. On the Hanukkah Menorah, the **shamash** candle is often higher than the others, or distinguished in some way, yet it is truly the most humble of the candles. It isn't counted among those required to be lit each night and its sole purpose is to light the other candles. There is no miracle associated with the **shamash**. It is merely functional.

Similarly, the **shammes** who worked in the *shul*[17] in the old country was a low-level functionary. Not necessarily learned, not a rabbi nor a teacher, the **shammes** ensured that the heat and lights were turned on before the services began, and that the building was locked after the services ended. He also collected and distributed the *tzedakah*[18] and assigned the honors on Torah reading days. The **shammes** knew who was commemorating the death of a parent on a particular day and offered him an honor or role in the service. The **shammes** passed along those honors to others without ever reserving one for himself.

When I graduated from the Jewish Theological Seminary and was ordained as a rabbi, I was honored to have my grandmother's youngest brother, my Uncle Shalom of blessed memory, attend the ceremony. He had once served as a **shammes**, and was the only one of his generation still alive then – living on the Upper East Side of Manhattan, a convenient cab ride from the Seminary. He was so proud that I would be carrying on the family tradition of working in a synagogue, even though I had chosen the path of higher learning rather than that of the **shammes**. Many of us graduating that day believed that we would, in the rabbinate, answer a higher calling by serving God and our communities. Over the years, I have come to appreciate that collecting and distributing charitable funds, offering

---

[17] Synagogue. See page 59.

[18] *Tzedakah* is the word used for charity or funds collected for charity, but this is not a literal translation. Unlike the English word charity, which derives from the Latin root "to care or value," *tzedakah* comes from the Hebrew root which signifies righteousness or justice.

honor to others in the community, and eschewing public acknow-
ledgments of my successes in the rabbinate are the most worthy pursuits
of my profession and best honor the memory of our family's **shammes**.

The lesson of the **shamash** is that serving is about making the light
of others shine more brightly. It is a simple, humbling lesson – one
that we must revisit often, reminding ourselves to cherish light of the
shammes along with the other candles.

Shiva (Hebrew) שבעה [sheev-**ah**] (often pronounced **shiv**-ah, as in Yiddish) *noun:* period of seven days of mourning (*literally:* seven)

Traditional Jews are professional mourners – we have been mourning the destruction of the Second Temple since the year 70 and entreating God to rebuild it at every opportunity in daily prayer, from silent meditations to the grace after meals. Some Jews leave a corner of their houses unpainted to symbolize that life without our holy Temple is incomplete. At his own wedding, the groom stomps on a glass, shattering the happiness of the occasion to remind all assembled that we live in a continual state of communal mourning.

Jews mourn collectively, at public funerals and burial ceremonies, where professional wailers were once paid to accompany the body to its final resting place. While cemetery workers usually lower the coffin, the immediate family is responsible for covering it with dirt, and friends usually take turns with a shovel until the grave is entirely filled. Then we "sit **shiva**." We spend seven days at home receiving visitors, talking about the life of the deceased, sharing stories and photographs, praying with a *minyan*[19] and reciting the mourner's prayer, known as the *Kaddish*. I almost forgot to mention that during **shiva** we eat... constantly. People bring cakes and casseroles, catered and home-cooked meals. The community provides calories along with comfort to the mourners, so they won't need to worry about mundane concerns such as preparing food for the week.

Throughout my years as a rabbi, people have often asked me about the proper etiquette when visiting a "**shiva** home," also referred to as paying a "**shiva** call." First, it is customary to walk right into the home without knocking or ringing the doorbell. Then offer condolences to the mourners and sit with them. The traditional greeting is "May you be comforted among those who mourn for Zion and Jerusalem." Always follow the lead of the mourners – know that your silent presence offers consolation. It is appropriate to share a story or memory if you knew the deceased, but do not try to cheer the mourners or distract them from their sorrow. **Shiva** is a time for embracing grief and cherishing memories. If you feel self-conscious at a **shiva** call, you are not alone! To ease the awkwardness, offer to bring the mourners a drink or snack or ask to see a photo. These

---

[19] The quorum required for public prayer.

gestures of kindness allow the mourners to get their needs met while giving you "something useful to do."

It is not always practical to make a **shiva** call – sometimes the burial and **shiva** are not observed locally, or for only a few days, because the **shiva** is cut short by holidays. Some Jews observe **shiva** for only three days, rather than the traditional seven. In such cases, it is appropriate to send a card or make a donation in memory of the deceased. However, phone calls are discouraged during **shiva**, as the mourner is not expected to have social contact and may not wish to speak on the phone.

When leaving the shiva home, rather than goodbye we say *rov simchas*, which loosely translates as "may we often meet at happy occasions." With nearly 2,000 years of mourning experience, Jews are also professional optimists.

Shul (Yiddish) שׁוּל [shool]
noun: school, synagogue (*variant spelling:* shule)

    Shul is such a great Yiddish word – not only is it shorter and easier to pronounce than "synagogue," it conveys so much meaning in one syllable. While the English word synagogue is derived from the Greek word for assembly or gathering, and the Hebrew phrase for synagogue, *bet knesset*, means literally house of assembly, **shul**'s origin is in the house of study. Gathering for prayer services and lunch is about getting together. Going to **shul** is about opening the heart and mind to Torah.

    The connection between study and the recitation of public prayers is long-standing. The ancient rabbis would begin and end their studies with blessings. Throughout the ages, the **shul** was a meeting place for the *minyan*, as well as the Jewish library and religious school. Much of the liturgy is fashioned around the recitation and study of biblical texts. The public reading of the Torah – a centerpiece of the Shabbat morning service – was originally meant to serve as an educational opportunity. **Shul** and study are intertwined and inseparable.

    In his introduction to *Sefer HaHinuch*, a medieval code of Jewish Law and commentary on the weekly Torah portions, the anonymous author shared his intentions for writing the book. It seems that in his day, youngsters were not sitting quietly in **shul** following along with the Torah reading. Instead, they were running wild in the courtyard and losing touch with their Jewish studies. I cannot confirm that his book solved the problem, since I do recall another rabbi mentioning – some eight centuries later – that the kids were often not in the sanctuary on the High Holidays. Yet the author of *Sefer HaHinuch* provided generations of **shul**-goers and rabbis insights into the weekly Torah portions. A colleague, who explained to me that his **shul**'s tradition was for the young people to congregate on the front steps during the lengthy High Holiday services, made a point of saying that he was glad that they were in attendance, if not in the building. In his mind, the power of prayer and study permeated the **shul** property.

    Shul conjures up a different image in my mind from synagogue. Perhaps it is the warmth of nostalgia for the more intimate **shul** of my grandparents' generation. It is certainly my natural bias as a teacher which leads me to **shul,** an extension of the school environment. **Shul** is where I best connect to God, by connecting to others who are engaged in Torah study.

Tachlis (Yiddish) תכלית [**takh**-liss]

noun: result, serious business, practical purpose

The holiday of Sukkot, on which we are commanded to live in a temporary structure called a *sukkah* (booth or hut), always reminds me of the word **tachlis**, which is one of those Yiddish words that almost can't be translated. **Tachlis** is what you accomplish after you have finished talking about doing it. **Tachlis** refers to the nuts-and-bolts, the logistics, the rolling up of sleeves and getting dirty if necessary. "Let's get started on **tachlis**," is what you say when you are ready to put the nail in the wall and hang the picture. I like getting to the **tachlis**, because it is at this stage of a process that we can enjoy the results of our work.

Building our family's *sukkah* is an extended project, and the work divides along what might be considered "traditional" gender lines. My husband *shleps* the wood beams and lattice walls from the garage to the back porch, climbs over the railing and hangs precariously from one arm as he attaches the outer wall. Our son watches, handing his father tools and eagerly awaiting that far-off day when it will be his turn to climb the ladder. Once the bamboo roof is secured, I painstakingly hang the dozens of decorations created by our daughters when they were so much younger, laminated and saved from year to year. The end result, a gorgeous temporary home, is reached just moments before the holiday arrives at sunset.

While **tachlis** is a necessary stage of any project, we also need the *reishis*, which is "the first place" or "beginning." If you don't know where and how to begin the work, if you don't devise a workable plan, you'll never get to the **tachlis**. I have been thinking a lot about the *reishis*, wondering what occupies "the first place" of Sukkot. On this holiday, as on many others, we invite friends and extended family to join us for meals. On Sukkot, unlike other holidays, we eat our meals in the *sukkah*, squeezing as many people as possible around the folding table in our temporary dining room. Together we conjure up images of famous guests we wish that we could entertain in our *sukkah*, if only they were not biblical heroes, deceased U.S. presidents, baseball greats and scientists of a bygone era. As we sit for hours, cramped in folding chairs, celebrating our connection to each other and to generations past, the walls of the *sukkah* seem to expand, suggesting that the *reishis* of Sukkot is relationships. Indeed, nurturing relationships is our *reishis* throughout the year, not only on holidays and special occasions. Knowing that we care about one another and are trying to achieve common goals, believing that it is important to greet each other with kind words and to connect on a personal level – this is our starting point. When we begin with our commitment to one another, our end result will be measurable progress.

Sukkot is known as the "time of our joy." The **tachlis** of the holiday is building the physical structure of the *sukkah*, but the joy of the holiday comes from the *reishis* of nurturing relationships in our temporary home. The *sukkah* is both sturdy and vulnerable – its roof is loosely bound and its interior is exposed to the elements – making it an apt symbol of our relationships. It embodies our ephemeral joy, allows us to dwell in the fleeting moment of the holiday. And when the holiday ends, so begins the **tachlis** of dismantling and storing the *sukkah* until next year.

Teshuvah (Hebrew) תשובה [t'shoo-**vah**]

noun: repentance, return

Every morning when my daughter comes downstairs for breakfast and I ask her "What'll it be?" she answers "The usual." Having worked as a waitress in a NJ diner in a previous life, I was familiar with this routine long before my child instituted it in my own home. Why does she eat the same breakfast five days a week? That's easy: We human beings are creatures of habit. Familiar routines feel comfortable and comforting to us in an ever-changing and uncertain world.

Given this tendency, what is the human capacity for **teshuvah**? Since true repentance requires change, it would seem that we are disinclined to repent. Maimonides[20] breaks down **teshuvah** into several steps: First, recognition of one's wrongdoing, followed by an apology to the wronged person and restitution when appropriate. Finally, a person must resolve not to repeat the mistake. The problem with achieving **teshuvah** is that we tend to fall back into familiar patterns of behavior even when they proved self-destructive in the first place. Moreover, we are unlikely to change our beliefs about ourselves and others, even though we reserve the right to change our minds, our fashion choices and our tastes on a regular basis. If **teshuvah** is impossible, or just improbable, why reserve the holiest days of the Jewish calendar for such a futile endeavor?

Perhaps we can learn a lesson about repentance from the second meaning of the word **teshuvah**: to return. In the context of repentance, it would not be logical to return to one's previous behavior. **Teshuvah** cannot be about returning to repeat our mistakes. Instead, its essence could be to return to a more pure state of being, to return to the Garden of Eden before mistakes were ever invented. We long to return to a simpler time, when we were free to be human beings yet unburdened by the need to repair a broken world and our broken selves. **Teshuvah** is a return to the beginning when the world was whole, when we were first created, blameless and without sin. It is a return to a wholeness of the spirit; it is a rebirth of the soul.

---

[20] Moses Maimonides (1135-1204) was a rabbi, physician, and Jewish philosopher in Spain and Egpyt during the Middle Ages. He is also known by the Hebrew acronym Rambam, which stands for **R**abbi **M**oses **b**en **M**aimon.

Talmud Torah
Lifelong Learning

Al regel aḥat (Hebrew) עַל רֶגֶל אַחַת [ahl reh-gell ah-ḥat]
colloquial: quickly, abbreviated, without commentary (*literally*: "on one foot")

My dean in rabbinical school kept a reminder taped to the filing cabinet in his office, a pithy quotation of Mark Twain: "No sinner was ever saved after the first twenty minutes of a sermon." Similarly, our homiletics professor, who had recently retired from the pulpit, beseeched us to refrain from delivering what he called "salad-bowl sermons," filled with iceberg lettuce and of limited nutritional value. Instead, he instructed us to give our congregants "one, ripe, juicy tomato." This, he insisted, they would always find satisfying.

The sage advice of my teachers originated with Hillel, a first-century rabbi whose penchant for keeping his lessons short-and-sweet is best illustrated in the following story: A non-Jew approaches Shammai, reputed be a brilliant but strict and humorless teacher, and asks the rabbi to teach him the whole Torah while standing on one foot. According to legend, Shammai chases his potential student away with a stick. Then the non-Jew approaches Hillel, who patiently gives the **al regel aḥat** answer: "That which is hateful to you do not do to your neighbor. The rest is commentary – go and learn."

Hillel's genius was his ability to distill the entire Torah down to one essential lesson. Despite his eloquence and brevity, most people remember only the beginning of Hillel's statement and often misquote him as having said "love your neighbor as yourself." But what Hillel said is more profound, because the end of his answer acknowledges the limitations of teaching **al regel aḥat**. Hillel understood that the enduring lessons of the Torah are not bland and cannot be gulped down while preoccupied with other matters. Rather, Torah study is a feast, served one delicious course at a time so that the student can savor every morsel. A taste of Torah should linger, and inspire a person to return for another meal, to order every item on the menu. My professors urged us modern rabbis to impart this lesson. I can give you a tomato while you stand on one foot, but you'll have to sit down to eat the rest of the meal on your own.

People tend to forget another crucial detail of this story: Like Shammai, Hillel sends the man away, chases him back to the books, although not as dramatically as his counterpart did. Hillel's parting words, "go and learn," remind us that we must continue our studies until we have absorbed the full complexity of the Torah. One must never be satisfied with quick, on-the-spot answers to difficult questions. For this reason, the sixty-three tractates of Talmud are filled with examples of legal cases and complicated stories demonstrating that the best answers include a multiplicity of opinions and ideas. It is possible to teach a single lesson **al regel aḥat,** but the wisdom of Torah must be acquired in a lifetime of learning.

Too often we expect others to answer questions **al regel aḥat** because the technology-driven society in which we live demands speed and accuracy in our thoughts and actions. The pressured pace of our lives does not always allow us to ruminate, process, and offer the full commentary in many situations. Still, we are wise to remember Hillel's complete lesson that the thinking and learning continue when both feet are planted firmly on the ground.

Identity (English)

noun: the set of behavioral or personal traits by which an individual is recognizable as a member of a group.[21]

I spend a lot of time thinking about the importance of identity. Perhaps my introspection is an occupational hazard: As a mother, a teacher, a rabbi and an artist, questions about identity are always percolating in my mind. Is identity formed at birth or can we change it? If my identity is what makes me recognizable as a member of a group, then is it defined by others around me? Does their perception of my identity actually influence who I am?

Identity isn't easy to define, which is probably why my preoccupation with these questions is ongoing. I believe that we all have multiple identities, and they can occasionally compete with one another for primacy. On the High Holidays, my identity as a rabbi is enhanced as I serve a small congregation in Auburn, Alabama. When the school nurse calls because my son has a fever, my identity as a mother is the only one that matters. Our sense of self adapts when we experience changes in our lives, especially in times of crisis. An adult child of aging parents understands how her identity as daughter competes with the other commitments of her adult life. Similarly, happy occasions can cause us to assert a particular identity. I know it's corny, but whenever I vote in an election I celebrate my identity as an American citizen.

Teachers and parents, especially those with toddlers or teenagers, are deeply involved in the process of identity formation. Our children and students are in flux at those critical times; they are trying on different identities and struggling to define themselves as individuals and we are their role models and mentors. As a rabbi and teacher in a Jewish school, my daily tasks centered on helping students form their own Jewish identities. Some express Jewish identity through religious observance and ritual. Others identify themselves as Jews by participating in cultural and social activities. Some speak fluent Hebrew and visit Israel often, and may choose to live there in the future. Others are active in community service as an expression of Jewish identity. I believe that it must be the mission of all adults – especially teachers – to help children of all faiths forge their identities as global citizens and to ensure that they will not be isolated adults.

---

[21] The American Heritage College Dictionary, Fourth Edition.

Guiding our children through this process can be challenging, but it is not without its rewards. If we help them to navigate successfully, then we will enjoy the fruits of our labor for many years to come.

One discovery of adulthood is that identity formation is a fluid process, and we continue to tweak our definitions of ourselves as we grow older. Lately, I have been searching for ways to allow my identity as a rabbi and my identity as a potter to converge. Through my art – which involves transforming dirt into visually-pleasing, functional objects – I am inspired to embrace the challenges of reformulating my identity and incorporating into daily life the spiritual practice of recognizing all beauty in the world as a gift from God.

Kishkes (Russian) КИШКИ (Yinglish[22]) קישקעס [kish-kes]
noun: guts, intestines

Imagine my surprise upon learning that my favorite Yiddish word is not Yiddish at all! It is a Russian word, but I have rendered it here phonetically in Yiddish, because I heard it so often from my dad in my youth that I want to endow it with an honorary status.

"You have to feel it in your **kishkes**!" This is a kind of mantra from my childhood, a parental encouragement to try something new, to be deeply committed to goals and to work hard to accomplish them. If you want to succeed at something, you must be passionate about it and about your success. In English we use the expression "you have to taste victory" to connote the physicality of longing. Knowing something in your gut is feeling it so deeply that your insides ache – it is qualitatively different than processing a thought in your brain, which takes a lot of time, or realizing something in your heart, which causes an instantaneous flutter. Your **kishkes** are where your center of gravity resides.

In my late thirties, I decided to try something new. I had a desire, emanating from deep in my **kishkes**, to express myself creatively. I had survived high school art classes, ashamed of my drawings which lacked perspective, knowing that visual-spatial perception was not my forte. Still, I had always wanted to try ceramics and found myself drawn to the pottery studio. I knew that getting dirt under my fingernails and hunkering down over a lump of clay would soothe the unarticulated stress burning in my **kishkes**.

My years at the pottery wheel have taught me patience and humility, and have confirmed for me some things I already knew about myself and about life. Achieving change, with regard to shaping the clay or determining one's path, requires firm but gentle pressure. I use my whole body, channeling not just the strength in my hands and arms, but also my upper back and shoulders, lower back, legs, even my jaw, when I work at the potter's wheel. It's called "throwing," and it demands all of me. To center the clay on the wheel, I extend my left arm to the clay, anchoring my elbow to my abdomen, grasping my left thumb with my right hand, applying steady pressure as I externalize the strength at my core, my center, my **kishkes**.

To test whether I have succeeded, I must close my eyes and steady my breathing. Then I touch the outer edge of the clay as it

---

[22] A mishmash of Yiddish and English, from Leo Rosten's *The Joys of Yinglish.*

spins, barely skimming it with the tips of my fingers. In a moment of utter silence and stillness, I listen by touching, I see by feeling. It is a spiritual moment, as an earnest prayer inhabits my **kishkes**. The clay is centered, and I am ready to create a beautiful vessel from a lump of dirt. Like God created humanity, breathing a passionate soul into the dust of the earth. I am the beautiful vessel; my artistic soul spreads through my body, and I feel it at the core. I feel it in my **kishkes**.

Kulmus (Hebrew) קולמוס [**kool**-moose]
noun: writing quill, reed pen, from the Latin *calamus*

Many years ago I had the privilege of watching the steady hand of a Sofer[23] completing the final letters in a Torah. It was a religious experience. His **kulmus** never wavered; instead he formed each letter carefully, turning the **kulmus** only slightly to produce the desired thickness of each segment of each letter. It was as though the tool became one with his hand. The grace of his movements as he adorned the letters with their crowns suggested that the **kulmus**, literally light as a feather in his hands, was the perfect writing instrument.

Once, I thought about picking up the **kulmus** myself. Because I am left-handed, it was not until I learned to write in Hebrew that I was able to write in ink without smudging the letters. Since it is written from right to left, Hebrew calligraphy was a breeze, as I was able to slide my left hand across the page away from the drying ink. As a teenager, I wrote prayers and sections of Torah in Hebrew calligraphy, decorating the pages with original artwork. For years I longed to apprentice with a scribe and write a Torah of my own.

These days, I rarely pick up my calligraphy pens anymore. There is no need for the **kulmus** when the Hebrew alphabet can be reproduced by computer. The beautiful letters of the Sofer's alphabet are even available as a font in most Hebrew word processing programs. When I think of using the **kulmus** it is with nostalgia for a simpler era, before my keyboard replaced my desire to write with a quill. The Sofer, however, continues to grasp the **kulmus**.

What is remarkable about the Sofer is that he uses such humble tools to accomplish the enormous task of writing a Torah. The **kulmus** is the humblest of these tools, formed out of the feather of a turkey or goose. One scribe I know uses turkey feathers exclusively, to remind him that one of God's least elegant creatures can make the most significant contribution to his work. Like a single instrument in the orchestra, the **kulmus** is essential to the finished product.

---

[23] A Sofer is a specially trained scribe who is entrusted to write holy texts, such as the Torah and other texts found in ritual objects. The Torah, or Five Books of Moses, is not merely a book. It is the central text of the Jewish people, and both a symbol and embodiment of Jewish law. Written by hand on parchment in handmade ink, scrolls of Torah are opened and read weekly in synagogues and schools, and are closed and stored in beautiful cabinets known as holy arks.

Sechel (Yiddish) שׂכל [**say-khl**]

noun: common sense; smarts; wit; tact, diplomacy

The early rabbis were adherents to the theory of multiple intelligences nearly 2,000 years before it was published by Howard Gardner. They understood that people have different ways of knowing, and they honored the many varieties of knowledge and wisdom that we possess. In fact, one of the most ancient and central prayers in the liturgy praises God for granting us three different types of intelligence. Among these three, I believe that **sechel** is the most valuable.

For some people, it's easy to memorize facts and calculate figures. This is knowledge that can be taught in academic courses. It is not so simple, however, to know how to apply a theory of physics to everyday life or to articulate an opinion persuasively. This is knowledge that is discerned over time, and with greater effort and maturity. It can be difficult to know the right thing to say when a friend is struggling with an ethical dilemma or to know when it is acceptable to interrupt a conversation. This is the wisdom one acquires through life experiences. This is **sechel**, and because it cannot be learned through memorization or repetition of problem sets, it remains elusive for some.

Sechel is knowing when to ask a question and when to answer one. Moreover, **sechel** is knowing when to keep silent. **Sechel** is knowing about people and relationships. **Sechel** is knowing what you don't know, and knowing how to learn it. **Sechel** is also knowing how to share your knowledge with others. When I was young, my dad was fond of reminding me that **sechel** was the kind of "smarts" that either you had it or you didn't, and you couldn't learn it in a book. He would appeal to me and my brother to use our **sechel**, because he recognized that even small children can possess tremendous intelligence in the form of common sense and intuition.

There are a lot of words for knowledge in Hebrew, derived from different roots, but the Hebrew word for enlightenment, *haskalah*, is derived from the same root as **sechel**. An enlightened person has acquired wisdom in many forms, and can use his or her **sechel** to spread light to others.

72

Senioritis (English)

noun, colloquial: decreased motivation toward studies displayed by students nearing the end of their high school or college careers[24]

While not technically a disease, **senioritis** does seem to mimic a physical affliction. It is typically said to include slowness, procrastination, apathy regarding school work, and a tendency toward truancy. Many high school and college students find themselves in what could be called a "lame duck" situation: Their plans for next year are finalized and a new chapter in their lives is about to begin, so finishing the current chapter becomes just a formality. They are stuck in a holding pattern, waiting to land with diploma in hand on graduation day. It is important to note that **senioritis** is not a medical term; it is not recognized by the American Psychiatric Association or any other medical body as an actual illness. While **senioritis** is generally viewed as an imaginary disease, its effects are well known to teachers and students alike.

In my second year as a high school teacher, I noticed that some of my favorite students had begun exhibiting symptoms of **senioritis** in May of their junior year, nearly a full year before their anticipated graduation date. As they completed their AP exams, **senioritis** reached epidemic proportions – the juniors were exhausted and the seniors had all but physically checked out. At the time, I accepted this situation as inevitable, and found it oddly comforting. This is the way of the high school world – if they didn't develop **senioritis**, we would really worry.

I wonder if there is anything positive that arises from this annual outbreak. Perhaps **senioritis** eases the separation anxiety that students experience as they prepare to leave their school and homes, at this particular moment in their almost-adult lives. By checking-out mentally several months before graduation, they have time to grow accustomed to feeling as though they have left childhood behind. For me, it has been more than a few years since I developed an awful case of **senioritis** in college – I couldn't believe I had to leave the bucolic campus of Haverford for the polluted city, and I wasn't ready to say goodbye to my roommates, my intellectual soul mates and best friends.

---

[24] For this definition, I consulted the online source for all things cultural: Wikipedia!

Senioritis provided me with a blasé stance that masked the pain caused by my departure – it wasn't a bad exit strategy at the time. If so many students did not already catch **senioritis**, I might consider suggesting it to them as a coping mechanism as they take their final steps from home, and their first steps in the journey to adulthood.

Talmid Chacham (Hebrew/Yiddish) תלמיד חכם [tahl-**meed** ḥah-**khahm**]
Talmidei Chachamim (*pl.*) תלמידי חכמים [tahl-meed-**day** ḥah-khah-**meem**]
noun: scholar(s) (*literally:* wise student)

The ancient rabbis pretty much divided their world into two types of people: **talmidei chachamim**, scholars and students of Torah, and *amei ha-aretz*, everyone else. They preferred to associate only with other scholars – they ate sabbath meals together, hung out at recess together – and distrusted the *kashrut*[25] of the ignoramuses, whom they suspected to be unscrupulous about tithing. So began a social-religious caste system in ancient Israel, as the **talmidei chachamim** refused to purchase produce from anyone whose knowledge and practice of the dietary laws did not mirror their own.

Yet, in their attempt to employ peer pressure to raise the standards of learning and observance, the ancient rabbis may have lost the original intent of the expression **talmid chacham**. In its essence, the word *talmid* indicates a person who is engaged in ongoing study, rather than a sage who dispenses wisdom to others. While the word *chacham* as an adjective means "wise," as a verb it means "[he] became wise." Nor does this refer to innate intelligence or natural talent. A **talmid chacham** is a person who became wise, presumably through study.

In my years of study for the rabbinate, and as an educator, I have studied Torah with many **talmidei chachamim**, most of whom were not rabbis. They are doctors, lawyers, accountants, engineers, computer programmers, statisticians, social workers, middle school math teachers, nurses, retirees and mothers of young children who are working at home rather than pursuing their careers. These adult learners – with varying degrees of Jewish knowledge and background, with areas of expertise outside of Judaic studies, with rich life experiences and emotional intelligence – are some of the wisest **talmidei chachamim** I have had the privilege of knowing. They are my students; moreover, they are my teachers.

Roughly 2,000 years ago, one rabbi commented that a true *chacham* is one who learns from everyone else. Today, with the benefit of centuries of accumulated wisdom, we understand that a true **talmid chacham** is one who continues to learn and grow, who strives to remain a life-long learner, if not a full-time student. A scholar is not an academician who has mastered a particular subject, but a student who has mastered the art of learning.

---

[25] *Kashrut* refers to Jewish dietary laws. Kosher literally means "appropriate" or "fit for use."

Acknowledgements

This book would not have been possible without the support of many people, whose names I hesitate to print here as I live in fear of omitting one kind soul who offered encouragement, advice, and help with editing and marketing. Still, I would be remiss not to mention those who contributed their time and talent to this project. There were several midwives who nurtured the manuscript from its infancy to the book you are holding in your hands. First, I wish to acknowledge the significant contributions of Corey-Jan Albert, editor, I.T. and marketing guru, cheerleader, and above all, friend. My other readers were Shelley Buxbaum, Suzi Ehtashem-Zadeh, Deana Linfield, Helen Luttrell, and Marnie Nadolne. They deserve only praise, since any errors that remain in the final version are mine. Finally, I owe a debt of gratitude to Rochelle Nation, whose passing remark inspired me to write the first essay. To all these women: Your encouragement, loyalty and friendship account for many blessings in my life.

It has been my privilege to serve as a rabbi and teacher in many communities in the southeast. Thank you to my students and colleagues at The Brill Institute, Camp Ramah Darom, Kol Echad Institute and The Weber School. I have learned so much from studying with you, my *talmidei chachamim*. I am also grateful to my friends at Congregation Shaarey Israel of Macon, GA and Beth Shalom of Auburn, Alabama, who allowed me to share my words with them in sermons. Thank you to the following teachers at High Meadows School, in whose classrooms I was inspired to write alongside my children: Sue Buffum, Suzi Ehtashem-Zadeh, Brian Ivey, and Chris Korb. Special thanks to David Barrack, Susan Lubliner and Loren Stein for donating their time and beautiful art to this project, and to Beth Levine for permitting me to print her *hamantashen* recipe. Thanks to my *haverim* who encouraged me to pursue this project: Audrey Galex, Saleemah Abdul-Ghafur, Rabbi Brad Hirschfield, Reverend Ben Johnson, Melody Moezzi, Rabbi Daniel Rosenberg, Barbara Rosenblit, Rabbi Jeff Salkin, Pastor Bob Sims and Zuzana Urbanek. Finally, I want to thank the staff of Office Max at Merchant's Walk for their patience and professional services.

I lack adequate space to articulate the many ways my friends have helped me! Thank you: Dennis Barrett, Beth Berger, Charlotte Brown, Maureen Carithers, Natali Ceniza, Paula Coplon, Ron Feinberg, Peggy Freedman, Denise Gelernter, Nancy Gorod, Rachel Hallote, Kathleen Johnson Hodges, Shari Judenberg, Dr. Brian Nadolne, Kimberly and

Al Reingold, Yael Sandler, Ellen Sichel, Miri Sternberg, Judith Swartz, Cully Veal, Marla Zimmerman, and Chari Rabinowitz Goldberg and Sheryl Stein, high school friends who reconnected via Facebook and immediately offered their support. I treasure your friendship and presence in my life. I owe so much to my parents: Mom and Eugene, Dad and Bobbi, Mom and Charlie, and Dad; and to Aunt Cynthia and Aunt Linda; and to my siblings, David & Lisa, Zack, Marlene & Avery, Lisa & Rich. To Maital, Shira and Jonah: Thank you for sharing Ima's attention with her "baby" and for allowing me to write about our life. For David, my *bashert*, I have no words other than "I love you."